75¢

BE ALL THAT
YOU ARE

BY

JAMES FADIMAN, Ph.D.

Westlake Press

ACKNOWLEDGEMENTS

Writing is never a solitary task. I've been assisted by the careful criticisms and suggestions of Jim Jensen, Lee Pulos, Kathy Speeth, Jeff and Mary-Jo Fadiman, and Lynn Yeager.

I am indebted to the editing skills and good will of Jill Mellick, who created order where there was none, restored my original prose to English, and made this manuscript far more lucid than it would have been without her.

I am also grateful to those friends, clients and members of my family, especially my wife Dorothy, who allowed me the time and the privacy that I needed to write at all.

Most of all, I am grateful to the openness and the beauty of those who have shared their lives with me. It is your stories that inspired me to write this book, and it is your stories which made these ideas real.

DEDICATION

To
John Boyle

Whose life was committed to giving to others and whose work restored to others the opportunities they had thought lost. John taught that there is enough for us all. He demonstrated it with his generosity, his zest for life and his dedication to helping others achieve their chosen goals.

To
Helen Boyle

Whose wisdom, kindness and good nature developed and supported me. Helen's understanding and myriad contributions cannot be counted; they are a continual string of blessings which keep the work always focused in service and on love.

* * * *

Thank you John and Helen, for allowing me to teach your work without hesitation or limitation.

Table of Contents

INTRODUCTION vii

Chapter I   **FREEDOM AND**
             LIMITATION 1
               Basic assumptions
               The structure of our mind
               Forming our self-concept
               Limitations
               The forces of liberation

Chapter II   **GOALS** 33
               Why have goals?
               Universal goals
               Basic goals
               Individual goals
               Developing goals

Chapter III   **TRAINING AND RETRAINING**
             THE MIND 51
               Revising our data
               Overcoming limits to change
               The paradox of the present
               The power and value of suggestion

Chapter IV   **HIGHER MIND** 65
               Conscious and subconscious
               Will and synthesis
               Self-actualization
               The higher self
               The higher self in action
               Other facets of the higher self
               Self-concept and the higher self

Chapter V   PROBLEM SOLVING 79
             Emotional blocks
             Cultural blocks
             Environmental blocks
             Intellectual blocks
             Perceptual blocks

Chapter VI   OVERCOMING BLOCKS 101
             A favorite way of thinking
             Active problem-solving
             Openness to experience
             Solutions from anywhere
             A direct method

Chapter VII HEALTH 111
             The mind-body connection
             Stress and change
             The power of words
             The problem of pain

Chapter VIII MARRIAGE AND CHILDREN .. 125
             Toward a better marriage
             Children
             Children and school

Chapter IX   AN END AND A BEGINNING .. 143
             What to do now
             Last words

SELECTED REFERENCES 148

THE OMEGA SEMINAR 150

INTRODUCTION

This is a book about freedom. It is about the basic forces which dominate your life. It is a guide to regaining control and opening up potentials within yourself which may have been closed.

It is vital to understand the correlations between your early history, your current mind-set, and your self-imposed limitations before you can correctly and successfully apply techniques which are appropriate to your situation. This book will give you that necessary understanding.

There are dozens of excellent books and courses available which teach goal setting. This book is a companion to almost all of them. It is a foundation for many specialized techniques which you may learn or currently practice.

It is an outgrowth of the Omega seminar, an intensive three to four day learning experience which has been attended by more than 30,000 people over the past 25 years. Never advertised, it has flourished through the referrals of those who cared to recommend it to their employees, family and friends.

The examples of transformations are drawn from people I've known and worked with in seminars, counseling, university classes, and other settings. No one system owns the truth.

If you have tried to improve your life before, (or are trying now) with only slight success, this book will help to clarify problems you may have encountered on your path. Taking full and total control of your life takes time, determination and information. The information presented here will encourage you to continue to develop your own path.

Freedom and a life that works are your birthright. Do not lose heart.

My own exposure to these ideas began in 1964 while I was a graduate student in Psychology at Stanford University. I took the seminar a second time after teaching Psychology at San Francisco State University and Brandeis University. Later, John Boyle offered me the opportunity to teach the seminar. I've been teaching it for 12 years now in addition to teaching part time at Stanford University and at the Institute for Transpersonal Psychology. I am also a management consultant, and have written or edited a number of books.

I am married to a gifted filmmaker; we have two daughters and two cats. I continue to teach and practice what is in this book.

James Fadiman, Ph.D.
Menlo Park, California
January, 1986

The greatest revolution in our generation
is the discovery that human beings,
by changing the inner attitudes of their minds
can change the outer aspects of their lives.
                                    William James

I

FREEDOM AND LIMITATION

If you don't start, you can't play.
If you don't play, you can't win.

Setting goals may be a simple matter, yet their establishment is only one step. Compelling concerns arise when you understand and confront the obstacles that can stand between you and your desired goals. Knowing the obstacles is the beginning of this work. Merely understanding the pitfalls is insufficient; we need to learn ways that problems can be overcome before goals become truly achievable. The route between wishful thinking and realizing our goals must be traveled with an artful combination of knowledge and effort. This chapter explores our current condition, as well as looking at the minefield of obstructions, difficulties, and disappointments which can prevent our attaining worthwhile goals.

1

BASIC ASSUMPTIONS ABOUT OURSELVES

The more we learn about our natural tendencies,
the easier it is to teach ourselves how to be good,
how to be happy, how to be fruitful,
how to respect ourselves, and how to love.
                                        Abraham Maslow

We all have immense potential, much of it dormant. We all possess gifts and encounter opportunities undeveloped and available. We do not know our limits as most of us settle for less than we are.

Biologists have stated that what is true for one member of a species is potentially true for any member of the species. That means that if there is one white crow, white crows are possible; if one redwood tree is 250 feet high and 30 feet around, redwood trees can grow as tall and as big as that. Anyone with a special gift or capability is a living indication of that same potential in each of us.

For example, the growing popularity of long distance running in the 1980's came from the dawning realization that almost anyone willing to train carefully can run long distances. Miracle stories pepper the running literature: People over 80 years old run marathons; a 54-year-old woman competes for a place on the U.S. Olympic women's marathon team against women half her age; people run across the entire country. Given a believable hope and the right support, we can vastly improve our condition and capacity, and transcend our previous expectations.

Studying unusual people serves to remind me that what I assume to be "natural limits" are regularly broken by people whose goals exceed my own. I think of my own memory, for example, as fairly good within "natural limits." But was Arturo

Toscanini's memory unnatural? He conducted entire symphonies from memory, knowing each note of each instrument in the orchestra. Was the memory of James Farley unnatural because as a politician he recognized, by face or name, over 20,000 people? Have I allowed myself to maintain a limit well below my potential capacity?

When I fumble over my checkbook or become confused doing my tax return, I may be consoled by telling myself that I'm not good with numbers. Yet I think about Nicholas Birns who, when he was five years old, would amuse and amaze adults by telling them what day of the week any date fell upon. Squirming and giggling he would announce that April 12, 1947 was a Wednesday while October 21, 1929 fell on a Monday. He was right of course, but didn't know how he knew.

I knew a reporter for **The New York Times** who could recall almost everything he had ever read. When asked to remember a poem or a quotation his eyes would close and he would begin to recite the passage. How did he do it?

"I see the pages in my mind," he said. "When I was a kid, I thought everybody could do it. I thought that's why people were so excited when they learned to read."

The facts are inescapable. Our species has vast potential. To realize that we have not reached our true limits is a first step. We need to face the parts of ourselves that created these limitations before we can begin to overcome them.

The nature of our self-concept

Who are You? Only when you know who you are, can you know who you can become.

Most of us have a sensible idea of who we are. We know our names, our sex, our nationality, our education, our skills, and our family history. We recall our childhood, our schooling, and the places where we have lived. We know how we behave and

3

what we have done. We know what we won't do, or at least haven't done until now. Often, we compare ourselves with others. We are better than or worse than so-and-so in this or that area. Our evaluation of ourselves may be high or low overall and is a composite of all of our self-evaluations.

Our self-concept, the sum of these multiple judgement calls, determines how slowly or quickly we achieve our goals. Self-concept is the governing element of inner life. A high self-concept is expansive; it supports us in starting new ventures, learning new skills, and achieving new goals. A low self-concept is restrictive: it prevents us from trying new ventures (I will fail), learning new skills (I am not smart enough), or achieving new goals (I am not able to set the goals I want now).

We each have considerable untapped potential. We also have a self-concept that reinforces personal limitations. **The level of personal effectiveness or the realized portion of your potential is exactly equal to your current self-concept.** In other words, you have become no more than you have imagined yourself capable of being. Your opinion of yourself eventually is accurately reflected by the level of your accomplishments.

The possibility that arises from this assumption is that if we can, in some way, raise our self-concept, the level of our achievements will rise as well. By raising our self-concept, our internal portrait, our external effectiveness increases. As Henry Ford once stated, "Those who believe that they can do something and those who believe that they can't are both right."

Self-concept is a critical governing factor in our lives, more important than family connections, educational opportunities, and quite possibly the governing factor in personal health and well-being. just as important, our self-concept is **learned**, built up over time and, while resistant to change, it can be changed effectively. It will help us to further understand self-concept if we can visualize a simplified structure of the mind.

THE STRUCTURE OF OUR MIND

If we think of the mind as a deep well, the portion above the ground is all that is visible. This visible portion of the mind is called consciousness. While it is only a small portion of the whole mind, it includes everything that we are aware of in any given moment. In school we learn consciously; at work we act consciously; in relationships we have conscious feelings and experiences.

Below consciousness, deep below the surface, is the subconscious. Much vaster in extent than the conscious, it contains all of our memories, which include a complete record of past experiences. It contains the memory of our opinions and our feelings about past events as well. The subconscious is not passive; it directly and continuously affects conscious decision-making processes. It supplies or withholds memories and feelings. On its own, it urges and demands actions not fully understood by the conscious mind.

How often have you said to yourself: "Why did I say that?" "What is so upsetting about this?" "What does that remind me of?" When you ask yourself these sorts of questions, your conscious mind lacks the data, held in your subconscious, to understand why you acted as you did.

While we like to believe that we act consciously, many of our actions originate directly from the subconscious without passing through the filter of our consciousness at all. Sometimes, for example, I notice that I have driven for miles with almost no recall of what I passed or how I drove. When we say someone is "absent-minded," we are observing that their conscious mind is preoccupied while their subconscious takes care of the moment-to-moment details of their daily life.

It was Sigmund Freud who observed that no mental process occurs randomly; there is a cause for every thought, feeling,

5

memory, or action. If "I" am not aware of the cause, this means that my conscious mind is unaware. However, the subconscious not only observes our actions, but is a major source of the intentions which precede and determine them.

How does the subconscious function?

Let us explore two ways it works. First, the subconscious stores memories. Second, it insures that our actions are consistent with our ideas about ourselves. We are never without a sense of identity. We never rush to the mirror in the morning to see who is there. We may wonder why we look so tired or bleary but we know who we are. We have a unfailing sense of personal identification. So strong is this subconscious portrait of ourselves that when we act in an unusual manner, we remark on the strangeness:

"Something must have gotten into me to behave like that."

"I'm just not that way."

"I never do that kind of thing."

It puzzles our conscious view of ourselves that we can behave subconsciously out of character, but we do. It is an endless game to discover the hidden habits, motives, urges, and memories that lead us to do something which, at first blush, does not square with our self-concept.

Where then does self-concept reside? It is a conscious summation of a great many attitudes. But even that is not the whole truth. The full self-concept is only partly conscious; like an iceberg, most of it is hidden from awareness and resides in the subconscious.

FORMING OUR SELF-CONCEPT

When we are born we are pure potential. The joy of young children is based on the lack of learned limitations. Everything seems possible to the unstructured mind.

Yet, as children grow older, as they gain skills, they also lose some of that initial openness. The first several years of a child's life are times of exceptional growth. At no other time do we learn so much so quickly and so easily. They learn consciously at first and gradually turn their learning into habits.

We learn to walk cautiously and carefully. Actually, we don't even walk; we toddle, paying attention to each step. Should we be distracted — flop! ... over we go onto our diapered bottoms. Eventually walking becomes second nature. Once we know how to walk, we can turn our attention to other things, such as where we want to walk, and what we might do when we get there.

Habits may support new learning. William James, the first great American psychologist, wrote about the value of habits in 1890:

> "Habit simplifies the movements required to achieve a given result; makes them more accurate and diminishes fatigue ... Habit is the enormous flywheel of society, its most precious conservative agent."

He was equally sensitive to habit's limitations:

> "Habit diminishes the conscious attention with which our acts are performed."

Habits that serve us are valuable, while habits that blind us prevent new learning and growth. Habits, such as walking, talking and reading are physical expressions of mental structures. To walk, a child needs not only the necessary maturity and practice, but also some inner statements such as "I want to walk ... I can walk ... I am a person who walks." Each of these statements becomes part of a growing self-concept. "I want" orients the conscious mind. "I can" reinforces the natural capacity to achieve. "I am" is a recognition of actual achievements.

Habits critical to self-concept development are built into early childhood just as language is built in; by hearing the message over and over again. Children listen in order to repeat, to

7

understand and to accept what they are learning. Most children eventually shift from constant discovery to occasional revelation. They lose the delight and wonder of seeing things freshly and learn "how to get along." They stop saying and imagining the unexpected and begin to say what others have told them to say. They learn habits of thinking, feeling, and acting which may constrict their potential. They learn how to survive — at a price.

Take for example the statement: "You're a good child." It is not altogether clear what parents mean by it. Slowly, as you gain experience, you discover which activities are considered "good," such as saying please or sharing a toy. You learn which activities are not "good," such as squeezing the cat too hard or dropping your milk glass on your sister. **You begin to act in accordance with what you have been told about yourself.** In a new situation you try to be good as an experiment, to find out if it gives you the results you wish. If it leads to parental approval, love, support and appreciation, you will tend (rightly enough) to do it next time. If it doesn't gain approval, you will try a different mode of behavior.

Our self-concept is created primarily through the ways we devise to gain the love and support of our parents. To young children, parents are the most powerful forces in the universe. Not only are they the major sources of love and security, but they are also the major sources of information, protection, punishment, fear and discipline. In short, the world of children revolves around being on the favorable side of their parents. It is not that whatever parents say is right; it is far stronger than that. Whatever our parents tell us when we are very small has all the power and authority of God speaking to Moses. There is no room to express a clear alternative to our parents' opinions.

It is easy to understand how we, as children, might learn to be good. We do something we are told that is good, and then we are rewarded with a smile, a hug or a toy. We learn to repeat that kind of behavior.

How do we learn a negative habit?

Imagine you are three years old. You are sitting in a high chair with a tiny plate and a small cup of milk. You move your hand excitedly and the cup tumbles to the floor. Since it is plastic, it bounces once or twice before resting quietly in an oval of spilled milk. From your perch you enjoy the play of white against the colors of the floor. Your mother, however, does not appreciate what you have done. "You are so **clumsy!**" (Note this word.) "You clean up your mess!" You are released from your highchair and you clean up the milk. Subconsciously you toy with the new word "clumsy." What could it mean? The act of making large circles of milk? The next day, you are back in your highchair with your lunch. Looking at your half-filled glass of milk you decide to recreate your artistry of yesterday. Over it goes; splash, bounce. Once again your mother (no sense of art) speaks to you. "I get so tired of your clumsy behavior. Clean it up, all of it!" Again you wipe it up and again the inner considerations. You're thinking, "clumsy ... um, seems to be a kind of movement I do with milk. Mother doesn't like it ... I don't like it either."

Days pass. On Sunday, in a moment of capricious joy, you spill your orange juice as you did the milk. Mother asks your father, "Honey, will you clean it up. Jonathan is becoming so clumsy." You hear what is being said about you and you finally understand. These acts of spilling are part of your character, part of the way you behave. Mother, who knows all things, has told you a secret about yourself that you did not know. **You are clumsy**. You are Jonathan Albert Dennison, you are three years old, you have a dog named Teddy and a teddy named Pup. You know a lot about yourself. You are a good boy; you are Mommy's little sweety; you are Daddy's favorite fella, and **you are clumsy**.

Being clumsy is no tragedy. It is one more fact in your life. It establishes part of your self-concept. It suggests how to behave; it orients and freezes a pattern around which a habit will begin to form.

Several years later in school, a new activity is suggested, say, forming clay on a wheel or rock climbing. You look at the activity, notice it takes physical dexterity and skill. "No," you say, "I don't want to do that. It doesn't look like fun." Inside, however, you are saying, "I don't want to do that because **I AM CLUMSY**, and I won't do it well." You don't learn potting or rock climbing.

In high school you might avoid dancing. "I don't like to dance" is what you say, but it is your fear of exposing your clumsiness that predetermines your answer. You don't learn to dance. As an adult you may not ski, or windsurf, or attempt a host of activities which demand initial learning and overcoming the clumsiness natural for any beginner.

It was not your mother's intention to have you grow up clumsy. Parents do the best job they can. Your self-concept is built up from what you are told directly, what is said about you to others and what your parents believe to be true.

Why do we as children accept limitations?

It is crucial to grasp the power that parents wield in our early development. **Our parents are so powerful that their opinions have the force of facts**. If your mother says you are clumsy, it is true! If she is sorry that you are clumsy, that is also true, but it only reinforces your growing clumsiness. Can you overcome it? Not easily, since to overcome it would be to put mother in the wrong. Nothing less than great effort will help you overcome your "natural" clumsiness. Nothing less than great effort will be enough, since you are going against a pattern deeply set into you at an early age by the most powerful people in the world.

The idea of being clumsy becomes a template around which related habits are built. It is an subconscious process. You become clumsy just as you become kind, generous, tidy, or attentive.

In a thousand ways, self-concept is created throughout our

childhood. Our self-concept becomes limited. What are these limitations?

LIMITATIONS

We are not free. We were born free, but are now hemmed in by life's curious mixture of joys and obligations. We envy the careless abandon with which small children devote themselves to one interest after another yet we lack their easy flow from tears to laughter, from play to quiet, from chores to games.

There are environmental limitations, physical limitations, even genetic limitations on our personal freedom. There are laws which prevent us from doing various activities, as well as economic realities which constrain us. All these are important and have real effects. However, we have found that the limitations which loom even larger are those we maintain in our own minds. They are portable cages, ready to drop into place around us when our minds demand it.

Horses are given blinders; devices to physically restrict their vision to a narrow strip of road in front of them. Humans are also fitted with blinders called limitations. What are the kinds of limitations? How are they formed? How are they imposed? How do we find ourselves willing, sometimes even determined, to maintain them? These are the vital questions we shall now explore.

Inhibitions

Inhibitions are self-imposed limits on intentions, feelings, thoughts, and actions. They constitute the fear of taking the first step. It is a **DO NOT ENTER** sign before an unlocked door.

Rather than admit that our inhibitions are rooted in our fears, human reason disguises them with laudatory terms. We speak of limiting risks, preventing failure, not losing time, or being adult about one's capacities. All these are ways to describe inhibitions.

To discover some of your inhibitions complete these sentence stubs. Take a moment now and try it.

> I can't ...
> I'm not able to ...
> I've no skill at ...
> I could never ...
> I'm no good in ...
> I know better than to ...

Each sentence you have completed describes your understanding of a limitation. Here is another group of sentences, less obvious, but which also evoke inhibitions. These sound postive and sensible, however, they are as effective in limiting freedom as the first group.

> I'm just being realistic.
> I'm nobody's fool.
> We all have to accept our natural limitations.
> You can't do everything you want.

All of us have statements like these rattling around in our heads. We all come to believe, accept and be tolerant of our inhibitions. We don't call them fears; instead we talk of the natural maturing process that occurs as wide-eyed children become more cautious and more sensible adults.

As a boy I went to a summer camp in the mountains of Southern California. There were large outcrops of huge granite boulders that I played on. These were separated by crevasses that I leapt across, as did two of my friends. We called ourselves "The Mountain Goats" and assumed that our capacity to make long leaps was natural. Twenty years later, I visited the area and climbed onto those same outcroppings. I was appalled to see the risks that I'd taken as a child.

If I slipped, the drops were 30-50 feet and the chance of serious injury was excellent. My willingness to make those jumps was gone. My loss could be called good judgement if you like, but the result is that I no longer leap those rocks. Call it prudence, but it looks and feels like limitation.

Can you overcome the unwillingness to brave a new situation? Can you overcome not only a fear of failure, but the effects of actual failures you have suffered in the past?

Of course you can, but first you need to understand the dilemma. Then you can work your way out of it — just as a trapped miner needs to investigate his situation before he can plan and make a successful escape.

We all have some limitations which inhibit us. These are not trivial nor are they illusions. They form part of our character, our personality, and our self-concept.

Compulsions

As an inhibition is a **DO NOT ENTER** sign, a compulsion is a **YOU MUST ENTER** sign. As inhibitions prevent you from starting things, compulsions pressure you to do things no matter what you would rather do.

While many inhibitions can easily be unmasked as ways to protect you from fear, compulsions are often more artfully concealed as virtues. Consider the virtue of neatness. It is useful to be neat. We can find our belongings. We don't create messes that might offend others, and so forth. However, let us now examine the compulsive shadow side of the virtue:

"I must keep my things neat and clean."

Why must you?

A usual answer is that it's obviously a better way to be. That does not explain the **must**. Underlying the must is a fear that if you don't keep things clean something unfortunate will happen to you.

An instructive exercise if you are a compulsively neat or tidy person is to imagine that, due to illness or accident, you are unable to keep your world cleaned up. Your home begins to be dusty and cluttered. Mail is unanswered; bills are overdue. As you play out this fantasy, your anxiety may rise.

In sessions past, when I've helped people to work with this fantasy situation their discomfort level has risen to an intolerable level. They asked me to end the exercise. Occasionally, the vague anxiety resolved to a conscious fear of impending punishment, usually including a cloudy vision of a parent. Sometimes the fear broke and erupted into laughter. The same vision of punishment appeared, yet when childhood conditioning was reviewed through adult eyes, fear dissipated and the compulsion was reduced.

Insight alone does not overcome a compulsion, but it can allow freedom for objective examination. Rabia, a colorful and perceptive saint once prayed, "Lord, if I serve thee in hope of Heaven, send me to Hell. If I serve thee in fear of Hell, send me to Hell. I would learn to serve thee for love of thee and love alone." She was praying to be free to the limitations bred by fear and its coverups, compulsions and inhibitions.

To uncover some of your own compulsions, complete the following sentence stubs:

I have to ...
I must ...

Everyone should ...
Why don't people all ...

We become compulsive so that we will not be anxious. We learned, as children, that it was worth the extra time it took, or the inconvenience to ourselves or others not to feel that anxiety. As adults we still act from concerns implanted during childhood. Our reasons have changed, but not our behavior. If we used to be on time so we wouldn't be spanked, now we are on time "so that we won't hold up other people," or "just out of common courtesy."

Negative habit patterns

A negative habit pattern has three aspects:
1. It restricts freedom of choice and action.
2. It is implanted during childhood and is linked to fear.
3. Because of the fear component, it is largely subconscious.

Inhibitions and compulsions are two major classes of negative habit patterns. A negative habit pattern is beyond control. **It behaves you**. Once triggered, it demands that you act. Once set into motion, it is difficult to stop or to modify.

Another kind of negative habit pattern is a phobia. A phobia is a fear that is disproportionate to the situation. It is so extreme that the frightened person even acknowledges its irrational dimensions. For example, you have a phobia about spiders. You know that spiders are small, ninety-nine percent harmless, and that most people are not afraid of them. When you see a spider, however, all that good sense vanishes and all you know is that **you must do something to get away from that spider**.

A phobia is a vivid example of a negative habit pattern. Almost all the psychological methods developed to treat phobias are aimed at helping a person develop the capacity to look beyond his or her immediate fear reaction, to the childhood pattern in which the fear was originally embedded.

In childhood we all learned, on the one hand, how to hold the love and attention of our parents, and on the other, how best to avoid pain, discomfort, loss of love and fear. We developed habits to protect ourselves. Those habits were the best solutions available to us at the time; however, retaining them into adult life has a price - the artificial restriction of our freedom and the damping down of our own capabilities. Why don't we release these childhood patterns when the need for them is past? We would if we could.

There is a fourth characteristic of negative habit patterns:

It is repressed so that the cause is not remembered. We do not like to experience fear; as children it is especially devastating. "How I can avoid fear" becomes a fundamental question for each of us as we grow up. An early reaction we learn is to take any action which will take us out of range.

We learn not to approach anything nor to do anything which increases our fear. We learn these acts consciously. Subconsciously we take a more subtle and more perplexing step. We try to avoid letting the conscious part of our mind even notice the threatening situation. We make the avoidance, the flight from fear, into an automatic reaction; a habit so well structured that it does not need conscious awareness. Just as the natural capacity of the body to protect itself moves our fingers off a hot stove without having to think about it, our subconscious habit patterns run us without the need to be aware of what we are doing or why. If we can avoid being afraid without noticing, so much the better.

A friend of mine had his feelings hurt when his parents told him that he had no talent for music. He stopped playing the piano soon after that. Hearing his own playing recalled his parents' negative opinion. He linked playing with the fear that they would love him less. He was less unhappy if he did not play. Thus he did not play. The result: no more fear but no more piano. As an adult he not only did not play an instrument, but when he was in a living room which had a piano, he sat so that he was as far away from the piano as possible, facing so that he could not see it. These were not conscious actions. They represented the progressive refinement of the initial negative habit pattern, to avoid fear restimulated by seeing a piano. When he was asked to observe his own behavior, it came as a complete surprise to him until he remembered the childhood events. He decided to overcome his phobia. He did not begin by playing the piano, but took up a different instrument at which he became proficient. He had continued to love music, but the subconscious need to escape from parental disapproval was far stronger than his conscious desire to play the instrument which evoked again and again his pain over their rejection.

As we will discuss in detail, negative habit patterns may be overcome by:

> **motivation**
> **awareness**
> **knowledge**
> **practice**

Then a positive habit pattern, conscious and under your control, can displace the negative one.

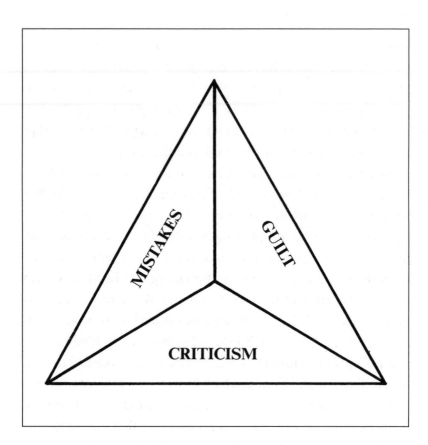

Mistakes - Criticism - Guilt

Consider this diagram. It is a pyramid in which each side supports the others. Mistakes, criticism, and guilt combine and interact to restrict personal happiness.

How do we acquire the burden of mistakes, the belittlement of criticism and the stinging scars of guilt? We are brought up by the expectations of our parents. What we are told about ourselves comes to pass. If we're told that we should be ashamed of ourselves for thinking, acting, or being a particular way, we become ashamed and strive to repress those aspects of our nature.

We may resist. We may became defiant and deny their input. We may even use the force of their disapproval to forge a powerful and independant identity. Usually, however, we do not resist; we capitulate to keep secure and to keep receiving their love. Just as parents who give their support and love have children who become loving and supportive, so to an extent do parents who make the mistake of confusing criticism with information and guilt with responsibility, lower their children's effectiveness. A patient of the psychoanalyst Karen Horney described the process (1949):

> "How is it possible to lose a self? The treachery, unknown and unthinkable, begins with our secret, psychic death in childhood — if and when we are not loved and are cut off from our spontaneous wishes. It is a perfect double crime in which the tiny self gradually and unwittingly takes part. He has not been accepted for himself, **as he is**. Oh, they love him, but they want or force him to be different! Therefore, **he must be unacceptable**. He himself learns to believe it and at last even takes it for granted ... and the whole thing is entirely plausible; all invisible, automatic, and anonymous. He has been rejected, not only by them but by himself."

Mistakes

We all make mistakes. Life is a series of opportunities to learn from these errors. Success might well be defined as a highly developed capacity to profit from mistakes. The lives of extremely successful people are peppered with mistakes **and how they learned from them**. Entrepreneurs average almost four failures before a major success. What separates them from others is their unwavering sense of self-worth. We test a behavior or an idea and if it succeeds, we are likely to try it again. If it fails, we shall either learn and try a different activity, or not learn and make the mistake again. If we repeat an unsuccessful response again and again, it may become a negative habit pattern. Both the event and its results are blocked out of awareness. A parent who says to a child, "If I've told you once, I've told you a thousand times" is a parent who has found a way that doesn't work. He or she repeats it, unable or unwilling to learn a more effective approach.

A common cause of mistakes is a lack of information. If you don't know that today is a bank holiday and go to cash a check, you will make a mistake. If you have a new computer and lose an important file, you probably have made a error in typing the commands. You gossip to someone about a third party; you find out later the two are old friends. Consequently, neither likes you for what you said. You've made a mistake. We all have examples of times when ignorance has led to our making mistakes.

Another cause of mistakes is negative habit patterns. These mistakes are mechanical and occur without your control and sometimes without your awareness. For example, during a job interview, you see a small spider in a corner and you have a mild spider phobia. You might become nervous and lose track of what is being said. The interview doesn't go well and you are not offered the job. Your nervousness is not your fault since you are unable to control your behavior.

Some people are labeled "accident prone." They have more than their share of common accidents. Things drop on them as often as they drop things. A few have neurological problems, but most have a self-concept that includes the conviction that, "I'm a clumsy person. I've always been clumsy. My folks always told me that I found accidents just waiting to happen. I guess it's true. I don't pay attention around stuff." With that critical self-concept, it should be no surprise that such a person has accidents.

Patterns of mistakes that are unchanged by new information are negative habit patterns. Listen, for example, to apologies. When people tell you that they are truly sorry about such and such by saying, "I just don't know what got into me," you are hearing a description of a negative habit pattern. They are truly unaware of their behavior and have limited their own capacity to observe and therefore, to change it.

We do make mistakes, and some of them happen because we don't know the right way or the right answer. We never learned, so we should not be punished or blamed. Some of our mistakes are negative habit patterns and since those are mechanical behaviors not open to consciousness, we should not blame ourselves for those either, any more than we blame ourselves for our height or hair color.

But the world often treats mistakes harshly. Friends, enemies, and most amazingly, we ourselves, hold up our mistakes and ask ourselves to feel shame, guilt, regret and remorse over these natural and inescapable events in our lives. "It's not my fault!" is a sentence we have all shouted at the world time after time as we grew up, pleading to be liberated from the stinging nettles of criticism. Our reaction and others' reactions to mistakes bring us to the second side of the pyramid.

Criticism

The word "critic" derives from the Greek word, to discern or to see clearly. A more constricted meaning refers to someone who observes flaws or defects. Professional critics or reviewers are supposed to balance their positive and negative observations and judgments, but they often damn more skillfully than they praise.

When criticism is objective, it can help correct a mistake. Objective criticism is informative, valuable, and can lead to improved performance, safety, and skill. When criticism is subjective and negative; fault-finding without suggesting ways to overcome the fault, we feel it as a direct attack. Such criticism actually lowers our subsequent effectiveness by lowering our self-concept.

Treating people as if they were incapable of independent judgement eventually pushes them toward less and less competence. There is a style of management which assumes that managers have to be hard on their staff, keep them in line, and chew people out when they foul up. This approach is losing credibility and is rarely observed in companies which are growing, profitable, or innovative. It is a low self-concept style.

We do make mistakes. We can learn from our mistakes when we are aided by informed, compassionate criticism. We will not improve if our critics are intent on hurting us, glorifying themselves, or fail to offer corrective information. To be told that we have mush for brains, or that we are one rotten S.O.B. does not serve us. It fails to clarify the problem and it doesn't improve the chances of our doing better next time.

To the extent that a child is criticized; called stupid, callous, selfish, irritating, unkind, ugly, dumb; that child's capacity is restricted, and his or her performance is diminished. When adults say these things to other adults, it has some of the same effect it has on children. The impact is less because it is one adult to another, but the capacity to wound and to be wounded is still present. **There is no evidence that abusive criticism ever helps anyone**.

Most of what we call criticism is not beneficial. It weakens the receiver and simply reinforces the tendencies which led to the initial criticism. People may improve their performance for a short time after being threatened, but long term improvement comes from praise and advice, not from intimidation. In addition, negative criticism harms the giver since it reinforces hurting instead of helping. By becoming more sensitive to the negative effects of criticism we can become more effective in dealing with others and with ourselves. A major effect of criticism is to generate guilt which brings us to the third side of the pyramid.

Guilt

Guilt comes from the Anglo-Saxon word "Gylt" for sin or crime. Guilt is a weapon and a dangerous one to use against another person. On the surface it has two functions.

First, guilt is used to control others. The French philosopher Voltaire once said, "If I can make a man feel guilty, I can control him."

Second, guilt is used to punish. Guilt hurts. It is an inner wound not easily healed. It makes another suffer long after the event. In spite of the apparent effectiveness of guilt to control and punish, a closer examination reveals severe limitations.

Guilt does not control. Voltaire was wrong. Guilt actually gives us permission and encouragement to perform the guilty act again. By saying someone is guilty of doing such and such, we are saying that this person is the kind of person who commits such acts. "I am a sinner" is a self-concept that can be maintained only by repeated sins. Thus the sins become permissible, since they are made part of one's self-concept. Guilt, in fact, encourages the repetition of the act since guilt feelings become an actual punishment. After experiencing and absorbing a punishment, someone is then free, having suffered, to recommit the act should the temptation reoccur.

Guilt persists. Pushing guilt onto someone scars the surface of their mind. Most of us carry such scars. Scarred in childhood by well-meaning but overly critical parents, teachers, ministers, and others, scarred as teenagers in our first fumbling relationships, and scarred again as adults by those who would use guilt to manipulate us.

Guilt belittles. It makes us ashamed of some aspect of our life. Guilt compounds a mistake, a single event, and labels it a character flaw. It becomes a permanent blemish in our mind.

Guilt spreads. People who are driven by guilt let it leak from one area of their lives to another until they live with an ongoing vague sense of guilt. It is as if the taste of many daily experiences become polluted by guilt. People who complain that their work is never good enough, that their goals are never met, that they are always a disappointment to those around them may be speaking about this vague sense of underlying guilt.

There are no benefits in holding onto guilt. There is no evidence that children who experience excessive guilt become better human beings. The removal of guilt is one of the great gifts that one person can give to themselves or to another. While the scars may not vanish, they can fade.

Mistakes lead to criticism, criticism to guilt, guilt to lowered overall effectiveness and to mistakes. In turn, mistakes create more criticism and so round and round it goes. Any effective way to change ourselves, therefore, must take into account these interactions among mistakes, criticism, and guilt. How do we begin to break this cycle and open ourselves up to lasting transformation?

The power of habits

Habits are the constant support for actions. If a habit propels us in the direction we wish to go, it is invaluable. For example, driving a car is a complicated series of actions which has, for most of us, become a set of subconscious habits. We don't concern ourselves with how to drive any more than we think about how to walk. By turning driving over to our subconscious mind, we are free to use driving time for reflection, conversation, or sightseeing. If we change to a different car, we become conscious of our driving habits for a few minutes; we rearrange our habits to fit the mechanism of the new car. Then off we go again, letting our habits do the driving. If the road conditions change from dry to icy, we pay closer conscious attention to the new situation. Then we adjust our driving habits, changing our habits for speed, passing, and braking, for example, while we continue to drive. To use habits well is part of living well.

Making maximum use of positive habits is the way to increase freedom and increase success. Habits can be created, changed, or eliminated and habits are directed by our subconscious mind. As a child we were less able to create or eliminate habits, since our inner and outer lives were dominated by our parents and our own desire to please them and thus gain or retain their love.

To modify a positive habit is not difficult. All of the information is available to consciousness. To change a negative habit pattern is a subtler procedure. The reasons for the habit, the actual root causes, are often repressed and forgotten. The conscious mind may not even be aware of the habit. Negative habits inhibit new learning, adapting, growing and changing to fit new circumstances. Effective personal growth depends on gaining increased control over our habits.

Believing in limits

A person is limited by what he
can hold in his imagination
                                    William James

What are the limits of human abilities? We have no real idea. We have established that few of us reach our limits. The Guinness Book of Records is a compilation of the possible. Every page is filled with the edge-points of human functioning. Each new edition lists hundreds of records broken and hundreds of new ones created by people who wanted the pleasure of being the best, the most, the highest, or the greatest in one thing or another. What is striking is not the records themselves; it is the changing records, the turnover from limit to limit to limit. Each one is a marker for the next record breaker. It is a book of limits asking to be exceeded!

In my neighborhood the high school track coach runs on his birthday. Every year his gift to himself is to run a mile for each year of his life. Last year, in his mid-forties, he ran an extra mile. "An extra candle," says he. When will he be unable to meet his desired goal? We cannot say.

Consider another runner, Bill Emmerton, probably the foremost long-long distance runner of our times. When he was fifty he ran 1100 miles in twenty-eight days. What are our limits?

The truth is that there are many capabilities open to us to use if we wish. One way to extend our ideas about limits is to understand that we can tap into attributes which appear exceptional by learning how to develop them. Instructors trained in accelerated learning techniques report that students can learn twice as much twice as fast as with conventional methods. Much of the training is unlearning previous limits.

Are there then any limits? Of course; trees don't grow endlessly into the sky. It is however, valuable to remember unusual peaks of human achievement. If our goal is to be healthy, we do not need to be able to run twenty-six miles in a few hours. It is energizing, however, to realize it is an achievable goal. It has been realized by children under 10 years old and adults over 85.

If our goal is to be wealthy, it is not likely that we need to be worth a billion dollars. There are a few billionaires, but there are dozens of millionaires in their early twenties in the United States alone, and thousands upon thousands of all ages worldwide. Some had advantages to start though most only had intention, information and a high self-concept. If your goal is to have a happy marriage, it is within your grasp once you learn how gently and firmly to grasp this goal. Our limits are within ourselves and not in the stars.

The process of achieving high goals is a natural part of the legacy given us at birth. Here we have emphasized that most of us do not use all our latent capacities. Later, in chapter IV we will see how another part of the mind is vital to achieving natural high-level success.

THE FORCES OF LIBERATION

In every effective system of personal transformation, there are four steps which lead to increased health, satisfaction, and a more conscious, productive life: **motivation, awareness, knowledge,** and **practice.** Details differ, as they should; each system has been created for specific groups in different cultures.

Motivation

We are all able to be aware of our own discomfort, but whether we can begin to change it is a different matter. The first and most basic step towards overcoming negative habit patterns and achieving a higher level of self-actualization is sincere desire.

We all know people who say, about their condition:

"It can't be helped."

"Other people have all the luck."

"Be grateful for small mercies."

"What can't be changed must be endured."

These statements lack the hope that things could turn around or improve; perhaps for others, but not for the speakers. Their self-concept does not include the possibility of being among the more fortunate, the gifted, or the likely-to-be-rewarded. They lack believable hope. They do not believe in themselves enough to begin to seek solutions to their problems, so their problems never get solved.

Your first step — and it is only a first step — is to acknowledge that these changing habit patterns seem to have been useful for others and to believe that they might be useful for you. However, belief by itself is insufficient. Once you have acknowledged that you want to make your life work more effectively you are ready to begin the second step; to become aware of critical issues in your life.

Awareness

To be aware is to be able to observe what is true in your own life, what has happened to you in the past, and what you wish for your future.

Awareness takes many forms. The important one for you is to notice, as clearly as you can, those moments when you are not free. To the extent that you can see the effects of repression, limited self-concept, inhibitions and compulsions, timidity, awkwardness, lack of ambition, and lack of faith in yourself you'll be able to make gains.

There is a strange and delightful dance that consciousness does with awareness. Your experience is the tiny portion of reality that you notice. Without determined effort, you do not pay close attention to situations which make you too uncomfortable. Thus, unless you are motivated to change, you may find it hard to expose your weaknesses to the light. Once you are motivated, however, you see clearly parts of yourself that were in shadow, and can consciously determine what needs to change.

At first, motivated awareness is like plunging into a cold, wave-battering ocean. The chill is real, but it lasts only a moment. Once you are in, opportunities to ride the waves appear which you couldn't begin to see until you took that first bone-chilling dive. Initially, it may be painful to confront opportunities passed by, self-maintained discomforts, or unsatisying relationships. It is not easy to acknowledge how you may have hurt your children, lost chances to be truly happy, or allowed physical habits or excessive work to erode your health.

To stop at this first step of awareness is almost worse than not starting. To make a list of all your household chores or personal obligations which need to be done and then to do none of them creates more suffering than ignoring those chores a while longer. Awareness is simply your tool for investigating your inner world so you may clarify what you would like to change. You can change any portion of any habit that you choose. The choices and the decisions are yours. By becoming more aware, you can make more enlightened decisions about changing yourself.

Knowledge

If you know **what** you want and know **that** you want, then you want to know **how** to go about getting it. The volumes of self-help literature, the seminars, tapes, classes and programs can be helpful although much of it stops at the first step. It increases your motivation, fanning the urge without giving you the substantive materials necessary to do the actual work. The cycle of motivation, awareness, and information needs to be repeated again and again as we grow. Each time we take a step up, we need to reevaluate our motivation, refine our awareness, and acquire current and correct information.

Knowledge that we can grow is not enough; knowledge that others have grown is not enough. Knowledge of how others have grown is useful; it is the vital link that activates the energy generated by desire and focused by awareness. Once you have learned what you can do for yourself and where to get the necessary knowledge, you begin to be responsible.

Just as awareness without knowledge can lead to depression, so knowledge without capacity to act can lead to frustration. Knowing that all you need to break out of prison is a rope and a hacksaw may not be of any help in escaping if you have no hope of getting either item. Knowledge should be approached warily. Once you know what is the right thing to do, you will be drawn to do it. There is a Chinese saying, "There is no such thing as an evil person." When asked to explain, this example is offered. Imagine a person who, walking along a road, sees a baby toddling by the edge of a pond. The baby loses its balance and falls into the pond. Is there a person who would not go to the pond and save the child? In a similar fashion, if your own life is teetering on the edge, and you know what to do to save it, you are likely to do what needs to be done.

Where you can find what you need to know and some resources you have to help you in your search are discussed throughout this book. As you learn the particular path to take you from your present state to the state that you choose, you will begin to transmute your knowledge. The responsibility to continue growing is part of what you learn along the way. Like a tree or any living system, no person is ever finished. Being truly alive means to remain open to new possibilities and new responses.

What then follows from knowledge? After knowledge comes practice. Indeed, help is given to those who help themselves.

Practice

The step from knowledge to practice is the last and the most critical step in changing habits. Just assuming responsibility does not seem to be enough to leap over the final hurdle from the original wish to the realized goal.

Perhaps the easy availability of knowledge has made us forget that knowledge is a middle step, not the first or the last.

30

Knowledge before desire leads only to scholarship; knowledge without awareness leads to egotism. Even worse, it leads to teaching others what you yourself do not practice. Public officials tell us to be thriftier with our funds while projects under their direction overrun the contracts. The balding barber knows volumes about hair care but not enough to help himself.

Moreover, much of what we call knowledge is only **knowledge about something**. It only describes the thing from the outside. For example, I can see films or read about Paris; that is "knowledge about." But how to get there, what to tell a taxi driver to get me to my hotel, what to eat, or what to do when the subways close, that is **knowledge of**; knowledge gained by direct experience. Knowledge **about** is good, but knowledge **of** is the real necessity.

Calvin Coolidge, who was known for never using an unnecessary word, came back to the White House from Church one Sunday. "How was the sermon?" he was asked.

"Good," was his reply.

"What was it about?"

"Sin," answered Coolidge.

"What did the minister have to say about it?" asked the slightly exasperated questioner.

"He was against it," answered the President terminating the discussion.

What Cooledge so deftly shows us in his accurate, yet useless, report was that merely being against sin does not have, by itself, any obvious effect. Unless there is knowledge of, we cannot act or make progress. The prayer, "Lord, let me know my sins," is a good prayer, however, it is not as useful as the prayer, "Lord, let me know what I may do to overcome my sins." The value of the meal is in the eating.

We must not stop with knowledge. Take for instance, a desire to become a fine diver. Motivation is the wish to dive; awareness alerts you to where swimming pools and diving boards are located. Knowledge teaches you to move your body correctly as you go through the air. Only practice makes you a fine diver. Practice blends your motivation, awareness, and knowledge into activities that succeed.

Living well comes from effective practice. Living a good life means to be able to see yourself clearly, your limitations as well as your strengths. Living well means that you are able to use your strengths correctly; you have the understanding necessary to establish goals; you know what you need, and you are able to profit from your understanding.

We begin our lives in perfect freedom. Childhood is both a time of expansion and a time when our freedoms become limited. Being truly adult means to take more and more responsibility for your own life; this demands motivation, awareness, knowledge, and practice. We should never lose the desire for more freedom. When the desire is conscious, the opportunities will present themselves. We are never without the tools for our own liberation.

II

GOALS

WHY HAVE GOALS?

Goals are not necessary for survival. Most people do not have active goals. They exist from day to day, doing what needs to be done, enjoying what they can, regretting what they can't. There are whole species without goals; they have their place in this world. Jellyfish are creatures without goals; they **literally** drift with the currents. When food passes close to them, they eat. When it does not, they don't. They go in whatever direction the waves move. Their life is an extreme example of living without goals. It is suitable for jellyfish and it works. They are one of the oldest unchanged species on the planet.

The decision to set goals is ours where and when we are able to make choices for ourselves. We are capable of leading active rather than passive lives. It is our contention that it is healthier to have conscious goals. Our lives have more possibilities than just drifting. To set goals is to use some of the extra capacities that distinguish us from jellyfish.

While we tend to see ourselves as having a constant identity, we are actually changing continuously. Physically, we lose
and gain millions of cells each day. The surface of our skin is
replaced every week, the tissue of our throat every few days. Over
a period of years, every single cell, with the exception of brain
tissue, is replaced. At the cellular level, we are in a continuous,
gradual process of transformation.

If you reflect on your interests and ideas, you will notice
that they, too, are undergoing gradual replacement with internal
changes, shifts, and reorientations. Like trees which drop their
leaves each winter to emerge with new, seemingly identical ones,
in the spring, we are in the process of change. We are, in fact,
beings-in-process. **We are changing, no matter what we say or do
or believe to the contrary**.

Since we are changing, having goals is a way for us to direct
that change. Since we have no choice but to be older, we can
choose how we intend to grow older. We can also chose to have
better health or worse, more freedom or less, greater income or
less, more relationships or fewer.

Maurice Maeterlinck, the Nobel prize winning author,
sums it up: "The more developed men are aware of their destiny.
They are familiar with their future because they are already part
of their future." Those who set goals create their own futures.

UNIVERSAL GOALS

Since we all had parents, were children, went to school,
developed relationships and careers, we have some common
history which includes a common set of internal goals.

The ideas of the psychologist Abraham Maslow help clarify
what is meant by **universal** or **basic goals**. He is best known for
his work on "self-actualization," a term he coined to describe the

34

highest and finest goals to which we aspire. He studied the brightest, the kindest, and the most creative and talented people he could find. He would ask them to nominate the most fully developed and impressive people that they knew. With this new list he would then explore and research the best qualities in members of that group.

Over the years he began to recognize patterns in these self-actualized individuals. They make "full use and exploitation of talents, capacities, potentialities, etc." While Maslow studied the famous and the gifted, he concluded by thinking of the self-actualizing man "not as an ordinary man with something added, but rather, as the ordinary man with nothing taken away. The average man is a full human being with dampened and inhibited powers and capacities." Self-actualizing people see life clearly; they are objective and are thus unlikely to allow hopes, fears, or defenses to distort their perception. They are committed to something greater than themselves and able to do well at their chosen tasks. They work hard and are spontaneous, creative, and courageous in their daily lives.

Self-actualizers enjoy and appreciate life more than most. Despite their normal share of pain, sorrow, and disappointments, they get more out of life. They have more interests and they also experience less fear, anxiety, boredom, and purposelessness. They are keenly aware of beauty and appreciate it in a sunrise, in nature, in their marriage — again and again. Most of us enjoy only occasional moments of joy or peak experience, while self-actualizers seem to love life in general, enjoying all its aspects.

Self-actualizers then, by Maslow's definition, are relatively free of neuroses and make excellent use of their innate talents and capacities. However, these people are not perfect. These "very same people can be at times boring, irritating, petulant, selfish, angry, or depressed. To avoid disillusionment with human nature, we must first give up our illusions about it," stated Maslow. Our so called natural limits are actually unnatural — common, usual, typical, but not valid; not the core of our being.

In his final book, Maslow describes eight kinds of habit patterns, behaviors which apparently lead towards self-actualization. Let us briefly explore each of these.

Concentration

"... self-actualization means experiencing fully, vividly, selflessly..." It is the capacity to see the actual situation occurring now and now and now. It is seeing with as few personal filters as possible.

Choosing growth

Life is a series of choices. We can choose to be safe, to hang back, to do what we have done before. On the other hand, we can choose to grow, to be challenged, to be stretched, to learn. Being safe carries the risk of regressing and shrinking back into ourselves. To choose growth is to choose to remain open, to be bold enough to look forward to the unknown.

Self-awareness

Self-actualizing rests on becoming more aware of our own inner nature and acting in accord with it. This means to be able to decide for ourselves what I wish to do, what I like, and what are my genuine needs. It is the result of heightened ability for us to be able to discriminate between external suggestions and internal realities.

Honesty

Each time we are honest and take responsibility for our own action, we move towards greater self-actualization. Posturing or giving answers calculated to please or placate others lowers self-esteem. Self-actualizers love the truth, even when it is unflattering or disturbing. They see the power that telling the truth gives them in their lives.

Judgement

As our self-concept improves, we learn to respect and trust our own judgments and our own instincts. Maslow observed that this trust leads to choices which are right for each individual.

Self-development

Self-actualization is the process of developing our potentialities. It is to work well, to do what we want to do. We may have great talent, but unless we develop that talent, we are not self-actualizing. The process of self-actualizing is ongoing. It is the never-ending process of making real our potentials, continually living, working, and relating to the whole; not only to a single accomplishment or even to a series of accomplishments.

Peak experiences

Peak experiences are transient moments of self-actualization. These are the times when we think, feel, and act most clearly and accurately. We are more loving, more accepting of others, temporarily free of inner conflicts and anxiety. We are better able to put our energies to constructive use.

Lack of defenses

When we can both recognize personal defenses and nega-tive habit patterns, **and let them go**, we can more easily act in healthier ways. One way, is to become more aware of the ways in which we obscure our image of ourselves and distort our view of the outer world.

How do these desirable self-actualizing characteristics translate themselves into goals? What goals are necessary and basic to all of us?

BASIC GOALS

The willingness to be happy

This is the fundamental note to which our whole life is tuned. It requires unwillingness to passively suffer, to accept defeat, to accept limitation, weakness, stupidity, and illness.

When you acknowledge a desire for change, the first step is to fully assure yourself that the intended change is beneficial, valuable, and pleasurable. To move from one poor job to another is change, but it is not growth. Suffering may be bene-ficial, but only when it leads, or promises to lead, to greater understanding.

Being willing to be happy asks you to accept that you are a person who deserves happiness. To deserve happiness means to have a self-concept which accepts your fundamental worth, with all your current and past problems, defects, and deficiencies, as well as an awareness of your potential, your talents, and your capacities. You cannot love another more than you love your-self. Being willing to be happy is not being happy, it just estab-lishes happiness as a goal. It supports the tree that sprouts from a seed of willingness.

The capacity to love

To be fully human is to be able to love. To be able to love more is to be more alive, more self-actualized, more successful at the game of existence. If you have already made the commitment to personal happiness, then a natural expression of that happiness is to take pleasure in and to appreciate others.

As happiness breeds happiness, so love and affection breed more love and affection. As children we may have been starved for love; we may have been frightened by and thwarted in expressing it. As a member of a couple we may be afraid of not receiving it; as parents we may not feel comfortable in giving it; as friends we may feel inhibited in expressing it. It is critical to improve our capacity to love. We find very little resistance to being more loving, but we are also aware that out of the rough-and-tumble of childhood many of us emerged scared, embittered, cautious, unskilled, and deficient in this natural capacity to love. We may confuse love with respect, with obedience, with guilt, with sex or with power. A necessary basic goal is to improve our willingness and our capacity to love. Like water from a bubbling well, giving love to others in abundance does not diminish the supply, it just increases the flow.

Good health

Some years ago I was in a serious car collision. I spent most of the following five months in bed. I couldn't work or fulfill my obligations as I was preoccupied with my health. What I observed was that I lost none of my willingness to be happy. If anything, the accident strengthened my determination. Throughout the period of recovery I uncovered opportunities for happiness that I would have missed in my usual busy, active life. I lost none of my desire to be able to love others. The accident gave me the leisure to see more clearly how vital loving others was to my own well-being and to theirs. Finally, I observed that without good health my financial, professional, and other goals lost their savor. There is nothing so central as the appreciation of our own well being. Whatever else we may think about our bodies, we all have a keen interest in keeping them fit, firm, and flexible.

There are many standards of health. As the willingness to be happy increases, goals for our own health also rise. Years ago a doctor told me, "I will work with you and help you to get healthier. When you feel you are healthy enough; when you wish no greater health, then you can stop doing what we have agreed on." What he taught me was that my goal should not end with "no illness," but should continue upward towards continued better health.

What are the basic requirements for good health? Physical fitness experts all agree on three:
   1. a diet that supports the proper nourishment of each cell,
   2. exercise that stimulates and improves circulation,
   3. the ability to relax.

When we are sick, our illness casts a fog over our lives. When we recover, it is as if there is more light; things take on a crystal clarity, and we have an increased enjoyment of each task we undertake. When good health wells up from every part of the body, it needs no definition, no intellectual understanding.

Inner integrity

Inner integrity is a subtle, yet basic goal. It is having more control over your own life with fewer and fewer urges to control others. The need to control others arises out of fear: fear that we will get less, that we will not be accepted, that we will lose love, and that we will be passed over. It also arises from the fear that others' defects will overwhelm our strengths. The need to control is a defense; rarely does it spring from positive inner feelings.

Manipulating others conflicts with other basic goals. The effort to control others is a strain which may show itself in physical symptoms including headaches, stomach problems, high blood pressure, and heart conditions. Trying to manipulate the world so that it will not harm us forecloses on love. We can not love people freely when we are on guard against them. We still love, but it is with one arm stretched out to embrace and the other ready to push away. Controlling others robs us of our inner joy. When we operate from weakness, without respect for our own capacity to face others openly and clearly, we diminish ourselves.

Inner integrity does not mean that we must speak out every thought or feeling that comes into our head. Neither does it mean that we allow ourselves to be pushed around. Inner integrity is the capacity to achieve what we wish in this world without limiting anyone's opportunities; it is also being aware that reinforcing others' integrity makes them our allies. At work we can delegate responsibility effectively; at home we allow each member of the family to be themselves.

It is from the foundation of the four basic goals that our fluctuating personal, private, and social goals emerge. As we begin to work on these basic goals, our individual goals become clearer and more attainable.

INDIVIDUAL GOALS

There are two kinds of individual goals: tangible goals, which include things like income, assets, houses, a boat, planes, horses, farms, gardens, and furniture; and intangible goals which may include health, skills, relationships, leisure, and self-confidence. The two sorts become intertwined, but it is possible and helpful to explore their differences.

Tangible goals

Tangible goals may cushion or support intangible personal goals. For example, longer life-expectancy in the United States is directly correlated with higher income. Being well-off does not improve your health, but being able to get better quality medical care may depend on how well-off you are. We live in a material world. It is easier and more practical to have enough economic support for our needs.

Learning to achieve greater material success has proved to be easy, obvious and effective. Surprisingly enough, Omega's results, to take one example, have shown that it is not difficult to teach people how to have enough money. Studies of hundreds of graduates have demonstrated that the goal of economic security is actually an "entrance goal" — a gate which opens up to reveal the goals beyond it. Once people overcome their fears of not having enough money, then they begin to work earnestly on their health, relationships, children, and personal satisfaction.

Intangible goals

Probably the most common intangible goals relate to family life. While most people can enjoy their work, their pleasure is enhanced if life is good at home. Many people may talk about their work as central, yet their long terms goals are rarely limited to work-related activities.

Health, of course, is another major goal. Setting specific health goals often leads to learning more about yourself, your life-style, and alternative ways to help yourself. Every physician can tell stories of those few patients who recovered despite the negative diagnosis, the severity of the illness , or the limitations of the treatment. Many long-term physical conditions can be turned around by careful and consistent goal setting.

A special health-related concern is weight. The goal is not merely to lose weight, it is to gradually develop a self-concept which includes sufficient self-control and the capacity to maintain a given weight.

Other goals focus on learning new skills and upgrading old ones. These goals range from learning new technologies to overcoming academic "weaknesses" in math or writing, from learning languages, to improving golf, tennis, or skiing skills. To be able to learn what you wish well and capably allows you to anticipate with appreciation the changes which are certain to occur in your future. As lifelong learning becomes more and more of a necessity, many people set goals to improve their capacities to be effective and productive students.

Individual goals can also strengthen character. To be comfortable in groups, to manage time more effectively, or to be kinder, more understanding or more confident are popular goals. For example, a successful financial analyst used to sit through endless presentations about new ventures, real estate partnerships, and other tax shelters. He wished that he could be as self-assured and as interesting as some of the speakers he'd heard. He set a goal to be a speaker in high demand, whose presentations were so stirring that he would receive a standing ovation when he spoke. Seven years after he started towards this goal, he had changed from being too shy to ever give a speech to giving thirty professional talks a year (turning down an equal number), most of which ended with a standing ovation. With a little encouragement you too can become an expert at creating worthwhile goals.

DEVELOPING GOALS

What should you consider before establishing a goal? What should you be aware of and careful about? These are important questions because the act of setting goals affects your future! You need to decide on a goal with one eye on the present, to be sure that you desire it right now, and one eye on the future, to be sure that the goal, once achieved, will bring contentment. Let us look at some of the critical questions to help in this process.

Do I truly want this goal?

How much of your present life is as you desire it? Are some of your activities only done to please or placate others? Are some done just to get by? Are some designed to adapt to others' goals? The following exercise ferrets out those parts of your life where you are not getting what you want. It may be a disconcerting exercise, but it is a useful one.

When you awake in the morning and think about getting up, ask yourself first whether you really want to get up. Be candid about it!

You take your bath or shower. Do you do it because you like it? Would you dodge it if you could?

Observe yourself eating your breakfast. Is it exactly the breakfast you like in kind and quantity? Is it **your** breakfast you eat or simply breakfast as defined by society? Do you, in fact, want to eat at all?

As you progress through the activities of your day, ask yourself: Do I freely choose to be where I am and to do what I am doing? Do I speak as I please to other people? Do I really like or only pretend to like some of these people?

Pass the day questioning — do I really like this or that? As evening approaches ask yourself: What would I truly like to do? Am I doing it?

The **doing** of what you like comes later. The important thing is to know what you **like**.

Do I want this goal?

It is undoubtedly virtuous to want to stop the desertification of vast stretches of Africa or to want to improve the living conditions of the homeless in our inner cities. However, if you do not intend to do anything about it or to get involved in any way, then it is not your goal. This is not being callous or selfish; it is not a "let the poor devils starve" position. It is a recognition that wishing on a star does not affect the star. Many goals are humanitarian but don't actually involve you. The initial task at hand is your own life. If you wish to be a force for improving this world, then first become more capable of handling your own life. It will be easier for you to aid others if your own life is a model of what is possible.

Can I express my goal clearly - in writing?

All too many of us have goals which are vague and nebulous:
"I want to be happy."
"I want to be successful."
"I wish things would be all right."
These are certainly positive goals but they are so unspecific that any progress is difficult to observe. To be happy is a positive direction, but the direction is much clearer if you can make it specific. For example, "I want to have more time with my oldest girl, to meet my sales quota without overwork, to lose my fear of going over bridges, and to control my arthritis so I can play tennis again." The more specific the goal, the more easily it will be achieved.

Clear descriptions of goals are important for another less obvious reason. We are each many people. These inner people constantly debate within us, polling their various interests about our actions. In each of us there is a parent, a worker, a lover, a liar, an athlete, a lazy one, a spendthrift, and a miser. Each aspect of our character has its own goals. By writing down a goal, we let it be reviewed by this internal committee to determine if most of them want it. If so, it is a goal that can be achieved more quickly than one which is buffeted about by inner bickering. For example, I can go to bed and my worker inside says, "Tomorrow I will get up a half-hour earlier. I will do some exercise, write those two troubling personal letters, get my breakfast, finish weeding under the plum trees, and place one call to an editor in New York. Then I will get on with my usual day." How splendid, I think. What planning! What good sense! I slip into sleep smiling. The next morning, however, is dark and cold. I recall my excellent and noble ideas of the previous night, yet the lazy part of me is snug and warm in my bed: "If I can get a little extra sleep this morning, I will feel better." As I turn over to go back to sleep, I wonder who it was who wanted to do all that extra work at this hour. I wish him well.

These internal dramas convince me to urge you to write down what matters to you; in this way, your committee can review, study, modify, and approve it.

Should I set time limits?

If you wish to double your income, do you really want to wait several years or is it acceptable for it to happen sooner? If you want to lower your blood pressure, is one time more favorable than another? If you want to have more leisure time to travel, how long do you want to postpone the realization of that goal?

In business, progress charts, five-year plans, quarterly goals, etc. are useful planning tools since they let you see what your intentions are as well as your guestimates of how long things should take. Is it all right to scrap these timelines if the situation changes?

Experience goes against conventional wisdom, as well as dozens of otherwise adequate and interesting systems taught to managers, business people, and educators. It is actually faster and easier and more attuned with the natural rhythms of the world **not** to establish time limits for your goals. Your goals are what you want **right now**. Setting time limits, actually pushes achievements off into the future. A corporation president was extremely proud of his long-range plans. He had made a plan 15 years ago to double his company revenues in five years, and he succeeded. He'd made another plan 10 years earlier to again double in five years. Once again he succeeded. A third time he set the goal of doubling in five years, and a third time he had been successful.

I asked him, "Would you be open to doubling your company in less than five years?" Some weeks and some discussions later, he agreed to leave his goals as they were, but he abolished the time limits. A year later he phoned and said. "I feel as if the world has become much less stable since I worked with you. A number of things came up in our market which we didn't anticipate when we did the plan. My managers felt freer to move quickly. We have doubled in the last year, and we have scrapped the original plan. I still like the way I used to work, but it is foolish to turn away superior results. Thanks for letting me out of my time limits."

Do not set time limits if possible! If you must set time limits, do so with your eyes open so that you do not confuse the possible with the usual. Goal setting is a game; the result of working without time limits is that you get to win more quickly and more often. Of course, this is simply an opinion based on experience. You will need to examine this for yourself to see if it can also be true for you.

47

Am I setting goals for others?

It would be wonderful if the neighborhood bully reformed and became a model citizen. It is more likely, however, that we can develop ourselves so that we need not fear nor attract that bully. It is more difficult to change others than to improve ourselves. It is not a good practice to set goals for others. We have neither the tools nor their agreement. Hoping that the other will change is a lazy attempt to improve your own life. Unexpressed in the wish to change others is a shadow of a low self-concept. It is a belief that the outer world controls and determines your happiness. The external world offers us rain and sunshine, full stomachs and empty ones, successes and mistakes. But it is not the king; it does not rule us. How we use what we are given is in us. Other people do not make our inner world; changing other people will not change our inner world.

It is generally unwise to set goals for others. For your sake and for theirs, however, there are exceptions. If you supervise others it is part of your job to help your people be productive and successful. Goal setting often clarifies the job itself, as well as the promotional opportunities available. You can also help your children establish meaningful goals. The less you intrude on others' goals, the more likely they are to set their own and chart their own future. People thrive when given their freedom.

While people agree that setting goals for others is not appropriate, they continue to pressure their spouse or children. They say, "Well ... they're different. I know them as well as they know themselves, and I know what will make them happy, what changes they should want to make." I am chilled by such remarks. They arise from loving concern, but they contain the underlying assumption that, "I am better qualified to run your life than you are."

My father hoped for years that I would get a regular job; a single employer, security, benefits, stability, and a clear career path. It didn't occur; he didn't push. I managed to be productive in a variety of jobs, and juggled my varied responsibilities. Eventually, as I became more successful, it became evident to my father that my family had neither suffered nor starved. He so wished to set that goal for me — for my own good — and for his peace of mind. Yet he refrained, and we both benefited.

A great liberation within marriages begins when each member truly respects the other enough so that neither wants to set goals for the other. Each spouse enjoys the changes in the other; each enjoys what the other achieves; each basks in the brighter light of a spouse whose self-concept includes the confidence and ability to make decisions which enhance their marriage.

Are my goals realistic?

It is vital to be realistic and to set goals which you can imagine. It is critical to have goals which make sense in terms of your life now. Remember that setting a goal also establishes that goal as a boundary. For example, some Omega graduates set goals to have a net worth of ten million dollars or more and have achieved those goals. For those people, those goals were realistic. Your goals are based on your current ideas of what is possible. What is actually possible may be much more. Therefore, keep it realistic. As your life expands don't preset limits; you do not know your own upper limits.

I collect stories which help me to see where my beliefs limit my ideas. Here are two from my collection. Draw your own conclusions.

Item I

Tim Agerter is a 19 year-old from Munster, Indiana. In pre-game warm-ups before Ohio State football games, Tim breaks downfield, cuts and leaps high to haul in a pass. He takes a center snap, drops back and throws a pass. Once in a while he lofts a short spiraling punt. What sets the fans buzzing is that Tim does it all on one leg. His right leg was amputated at age three. He sees nothing unusual about the speed, agility, and balance he displays despite his handicap. Agerter mastered his problem so well that in high school he was a competitive wrestler and high jumper in track and field. Not just an ordinary one either as he reached the state semifinals as a 105-pound wrestler and did even better in track, clearing 6'4″ in the high jump.

Says Ohio State coach Earle Bruce, "He's what you call a true athlete."

Item II

Ivor Welsh runs marathons. He takes 6 hours or more to finish, but he finishes. He usually runs first in his class. He was 85 when he ran his first marathon. Before I had heard of Ivor, I'd thought what he did was impossible. Ivor is not a long time runner; he took up running at age 82. Another fuse in my mind melted when I learned that. After a talk of Ivor's I asked him about his goals. His eyes lit up, and he said he was thinking of doing the Pike's Peak marathon next year. He was electric, excited, delightful, and filled with a joyful appreciation of his opportunities. Months later I opened a newsletter from a runner's club. On the cover was a picture of Ivor, smiling and wearing a PIKE'S PEAK MARATHON T-shirt. Ivor Welsh is realistic, and so are you.

These are ways to move toward your goals which work. It is critical to know your desires, be explicit about them, be realistic and start **now**. The next step toward using your full capacities is to learn how to rethink your habits and how to change basic patterns. Don't settle for less than you wish or less than you can do.

III

TRAINING AND RETRAINING THE MIND

We act on what we know. Only when we learn something new can we act differently. We behave as if our data were true and real. The truth, of course, is that data can be incomplete, outdated, even incorrect. We often become prisoners of our own information, unable to break out of self-generated errors. If we begin with false assumptions, the actions we take will be in error.

Can you recall a time when you forgot the first day of Daylight Savings Time? You went to work an hour early or late; called someone early or late; arrived somewhere early or late. All of your good intentions, careful planning, scheduling and organizing could not alter or overcome your mistaken assumption about the time.

Here follows an ancient example of this same problem.

Nasruddin, a Middle Eastern folk character, one day went down to the village pond. He took a container of yogurt and carefully spooned it into the pond. Then he stirred vigorously. His neighbors asked him what he was doing.

"Making yogurt," he replied brightly.

"But you can't make yogurt from water. You need milk," they retorted.

"Ah, but what if it works?" replied Nasruddin, undaunted by facts or the skepticism of his neighbors.

The problem is not that we lack the capacity to act differently; it is that false information prevents true freedom of action. When we become aware that obsolete data left over from childhood restricts our freedom, we develop the incentive to learn new correct information. New data can lead to new actions; new actions in turn can lead to new results.

REVISING OUR DATA

Is it difficult to revise personal data? No, we do it all the time. Our daily life is a succession of opportunities to take in new information. As we take in the new and stop using the old, we think differently, we plan differently, and we act differently.

For example, in April, 1984, the San Francisco Bay Area was shaken by a long, moderately intense earthquake. Within a few days, hundreds of people had called official agencies for help and advice about earthquake protection in the event of a stronger, more damaging quake. People wanted to learn how to bolt their homes to the foundations, how to strap hot water heaters against the walls, how to store emergency food and water, and how to shut off gas and electricity.

What was the new data that sparked their interest? It was not that they were living in a major earthquake zone; this they already knew. It was that they had realized that they **personally**

52

were living in such an area, that **their** house, **their** place of business, and **their** children's school could be damaged. Because of the recent quake, their knowledge was not only true, but it was current and vivid. A year later, laws were changed which forced insurance companies to clarify, in large type, what actual earthquake insurance was available. This second wave of information was a response to the renewed personal concerns about earthquake preparedness. Another round of information led to a another law which forced insurance companies to offer such coverage to every home owner in the area.

People, therefore, are open to new information which involves their welfare — **unless there are strong negative habit patterns restricting their awareness**. Smokers, for example, know about the health problems associated with smoking. Yet their habit is often too strong to allow real change. If you can see that you are **not** acting on information which could help you or make you happier, be assured that a negative habit pattern is running that portion of your life.

The process of learning and then changing beliefs based on new information happens in many areas. By way of example, new technology is often in operation before we have even begun to change our ideas about it. One of my relatives years ago came back from college declaring "I want to buy shares of a company called Xerox." She had been to the university library where for 25 cents she had made a copy of a single sheet of paper. Why buy Xerox? "Because," she said, "some day every university library in the country will want at least one of those machines." She was right, but her vision was restricted. Copy machine use expanded far beyond university libraries and changed the way business itself was conducted.

New data, new ideas, new attitudes, new actions, new industries, and new ways to work in turn generate new data. Once an idea is unleashed, it has enormous power to affect our lives. The history of science is the history of one theory being accepted until new data contradicts it, forcing the birth of a new theory. There are bitter battles between the experts of the old theory and the holders of the new data. Scientists are no different from the rest of us; their habit patterns can sometimes obscure their perception of reality. Max Planck, Nobel Prize winning physicist, once said, "My theories will be be accepted only after my colleagues are dead." It seemed an unfair judgment about the rigidity of his fellow physicists but history proved him correct. Some of us resist new data and cling to old habit patterns. Some of us observe the new and actively seek out ways to change.

As we observed earlier, effective development of new, more flexible habit patterns in our daily lives takes four steps:

motivation
awareness
knowledge
practice

These counter-balance the cycle of self-attack already described consisting of:

mistakes
guilt
criticism

Since early childhood, we have found success by wanting something, learning how to get it, and by implementing what we have learned. Observe, for example, the way a child learns to walk. Initially, there is the desire to walk, then the learning, and then the careful application of that learning. But there is more to learning to walk than the learning itself, there is also the emotional effect of each step on the child's mind. Learning something important always includes our reactions to each step along the way. Understanding these reactions can vastly accelerate our learning. As we learn new habits, the old ones do not vanish from the mind. We all have learned to walk, but we have not lost the capacity to crawl. Even more than our habits, our whole way of seeing and being in the world is retained, and stacked neatly inside our minds. Should we need to recall any portion of our past, our early memories appear to be complete and in order. An inability to recall something simply means that we have not pierced the veil between the conscious and the subconscious. No one has a "poor memory." It is a matter of understanding the habits we have been given, and no longer accepting the limitations to which we have become accustomed.

OVERCOMING LIMITS TO CHANGE

To what extent can motivated, knowledgeable people develop new habits? Most people can and do make remarkable changes when the situation is right.

I once counseled a young, overweight, belligerent, unemployed woman. "Jan" had used drugs for some years and had become phobic, unattractive, heavy, and sullen. She was too frightened to leave her house to go to a job. She had no relationships. She drank heavily, smoked, overate and she was extremely unhappy. At her request (intention) we focused on her weight. Because Jan valued the counseling sessions, I used them to motivate her. I told her that she could see me each time she lost three pounds. She wept and yelled at me that it was unfair, that she was in counseling because she couldn't control her weight. I stood my ground and she began to lose weight. As she did so, her capacity to run her own life began to re-emerge. She put herself on an extremely strict, sound diet for months and the weight flowed off her. As she thinned she became more and more capable of doing what she needed to do. Over the next few years Jan developed her own interests, her own job, and eventually her own business. The venture grew so rapidly that her husband (met along the path of her improved self-concept) decided to leave his management position in a bank to work in her business. Jan taught me that **if you give a person who wants to change the tools to change, the person will change**.

We do not know our limits. Consider smoking, one of the most dominating, compelling, and addicting habits known to medicine. When I teach I often ask if there are ex-smokers present. I ask if any of them simply stopped smoking one day and never picked it up again. Usually more than half the group of ex-smokers quit that way. Thousands of people have, by an act of personal courage and will, overcome their addiction successfully. That so many have done it is a tribute to the human spirit. There are numerous stop-smoking programs available, but none of these programs are effective unless the smoker has a clear intention to quit. What brings a person back to smoking after they have quit? The desire for the effects of smoking can be stronger than the benefits of not smoking. This occurs when we face emotional or physical stress. **Under stress we regress**. Smokers regress to earlier habits that offer safety, security, or acceptance and which include smoking.

Alcoholics Anonymous has created a successful self-help program based on **intention, information,** and **practice**. The first step in their program helps people acknowledge that they cannot control their drinking habits and that those habits are self-destructive. AA then provides information and support on how to change. They suggest that alcoholics who wish to stop drinking set a goal to be sober "one day at a time". Each sober day then becomes a time when their intention is reinforced, information is shown to be valid, and practice is experienced. Each sober day makes it easier to have another and eventually the practice becomes habit. To help people reaffirm their intentions frequent meetings remind the participants that they are working to develop and maintain new habits. The meetings also serve to remind members of their prior drinking habits and this way prevent denial of their faulty habit patterns of the past. Meetings of recovered drinkers encourage everyone of their need to maintain the new habits and new goals.

Intention is limited only by beliefs. For example, during a seminar a slim and obviously healthy couple revealed that each had lost over 30 pounds in the last year, reversing years of weight gain. A class member asked about their diet. Both laughed, "We don't diet any more ... it never worked. First we learned that we didn't have to be overweight. Then we decided to go for the weight we wanted. Our meals came trailing after us, changing to meet our new demands." Their first step was intention, the second was information; the results came from practice.

A businessman wrote me on his first anniversary after working with me. His income had increased 700% in one year. He was still doing the same kind of work and, putting what he'd learned to use, he had looked more carefully at his industry. He observed that people who were working for large companies, as he was, had safe, stable jobs and earned what he'd been earning. People who ran their own offices, however, seemed to earn much much more, though with occasional failures. He became willing to take a risk and his willingness paid off. Also, along with the higher income, he now works hours which allow him to take extended vacations with his family.

An old wise man once described life as an obstacle course — high hurdles, low hurdles, hedges, pits and brick walls. During childhood we are fitted with blindfolds before we run the course. Due to the fact that we can't see well, most of us fight with the obstacles, trying to go around them, tip them over, or fill them in. How much easier it becomes when we peek out from the blindfolds. A limitation is like a cold swimming pool on a warm day. Put one toe in and you are sure that it is uncomfortable; dive in and you are right — for a moment — it **is** uncomfortable. Then you discover that after the moment of discomfort it becomes a pleasure.

57

What makes us uncomfortable? Believing that our limitations are permanent.

"I'll **never** learn to swim/dance/bowl/skydive because ..."

"I **can't** get a promotion/new job/loving spouse because ..."

If we don't get past that first rush of discomfort, we can never find out if the obstacle was a mirage. Unless we begin, we cannot triumph.

Do we know what caused our particular limitations? Do we need to know in order to change? No to both questions. We have considered how limitations are created in childhood. Each of us had certain events, situations, and ideas impressed upon us which we incorporated into our developing self-concept. Childhood is a complex maze of feelings, thoughts, memories and events. It is a delightful and fascinating process to go back down the inner pathways into your own past to trace the outlines of the critical moments. No personal event is disconnected from the whole. Every thought, every impulse, every action, every dream is interconnected. In your own mind, there are no accidents; rather, there is an interwoven cloth of past, present, and anticipation of the future.

The first task is to overcome limitations so to get more of what you want now. When you have what you want then you can look, if you wish, into your early memories to discover root causes and to uncover the origins of your patterns. To look into yourself is to discover a collection of treasures. No one who deeply examines his or her own life can find it boring.

Childhood events are certainly pivotal, yet the details are less important than learning what to do to improve yourself now. Carl Jung, the Swiss founder of analytical psychology, came to a similar conclusion:

"We seldom get rid of an evil by understanding its causes — and for all our insight, obstinate habits do not disappear until replaced by other habits. But habits are won by exercise, and appropriate education is the sole means to this end ... No amount of confession and no amount of explaining can make the crooked plant grow straight; it must be trained upon the trellis ..."

THE PARADOX OF THE PRESENT

Let everyone try, I will not say to arrest,
but to notice or attend to the present moment of time.
One of the most baffling experiences occurs. Where is it,
this present? It has melted in our grasp,
fled ere we could touch it,
gone in the instant of becoming."
William James

The past is behind us and the future is unknown. Between the two, on the thinnest slice of time imaginable, is the present.

The experience of living in the "now" is as simple or as complex as our inner lives allow. Most of us do not live with maximum clarity or freedom as our view of the present is obscured by other concerns. The past encompasses not only our history, but also all of our past habits. It lumbers along with us into the present. When we act, we are not sure if we are paying attention to the actual present, or if we are repeating a habit pattern which is insensitive to the uniqueness of the current moment. Pressing against the present from the other side are our anticipations of the future. We expect one kind of future and steer our present actions to insure or prevent it. Should we envision a different future, our actions swing to a different tack.

An enlightened posture is to view our past as a treasure trove of prior solutions, events, ideas, speculations, mistakes and successes. We can draw on past habits to serve us in the present so we will not repeat mistakes. Neurosis is the compulsion to repeat mistakes; it is not only an an inability to use the past as a teacher, it is also the compulsion to recreate past problems and to reex-perience past failures. Neurosis is that part of us that hits our thumb each time we aim for a nail.

A friend of mine was married, then divorced, then dated, and finally started to see a woman seriously. He called me and asked if I could recommend a therapist. I was surprised since this was a man almost totally uninterested in his own mind. He had always said, "Life itself is psychology enough."

I asked him for his reasons and he told me that he was having the same problems with his new girlfriend that he had had with his ex-wife. "They are totally different kinds of people, he said, "so I think I am making the problem happen. I want to stop the pattern before it ruins my relationship with someone I love." He saw his past devouring his present. Counseling with a psychotherapist made him more aware of the habits. It supported him by suggesting to him methods to overcome them and eventually he remarried quite happily.

The wonderful revelation; the freeing realization is that the past is over; gone, finished, done with, completed, terminated ... IF YOU WISH! However, you may use past behaviors that work for you and you may leave behind the past behaviors that hurt you. New events can evoke new responses. Based on everything you've learned, you can fully respond to new situations. For example, right now I'm writing this book on a word processor. I utilize most of my typewriter typing habits. However, some of them are not useful on this machine. I have also developed new skills to gain access to the expanded capacities of the machine. A friend has offered me a newer computer for my work. Should I accept I shall once again keep some habits, modify others, and learn new ones.

Vast portions of our past are no longer necessary or even useful. The secret is to separate our valuables from our trash, then to remind ourselves to use the valuables correctly. The future is unknown. The way we establish our present casts light on our future. The future thus begins to shape itself in relation to our real present.

Freedom is too valuable to leave to chance, too rare to leave to past habits, and too important to let others establish for you.

THE POWER AND VALUE OF SUGGESTION

The word "suggestion" comes from a root meaning "to carry", or "to bring to." Suggestion is the act or the art of bringing something to mind. Suggestion is a powerful determinant of our view of the world. Although we may imagine ourselves to be self-determined, we can be as moved by suggestion as by our own inner urges.

Let us examine the role of suggestion in healing where we can see the complex interplay between the body and the mind. We find that the same forces, trivialized in advertising or propaganda, can be used to benefit others. If someone we respect tells us something, consciously as well as unconsciously, we tend to follow the suggestion.

An example comes from Carl Simonton, M.D. He reasoned that a patient might use the powers of the mind to supplement medical treatment. While this idea had been given lip service in his own medical speciality, cancer treatment, it was not then part of the normal treatment procedures. His first "mental help" patient was an older man with a large tumor in his throat. It was so large that the patient could barely swallow. Due to other complications, both surgery and radiation offered little hope. Simonton taught the patient to coach his own body to reverse the processes that nourished the cancer. He taught him to imagine his healing processes working successfully against the cancer. The patient did as he was told, fully trusting his young physician. Within weeks, the tumor began to shrink, and continued to do so until it was no longer a problem. Impressed with the results Simonton began to work with other cancer patients. He found that if a patient's desire to get well again was great enough, the information and the techniques he taught helped. He extended and developed his work until it is now recognized as an adjunct to many conventional treatments.

Six months later, Simonton's first patient called on him complaining about arthritis in his wrists, which were so painful and stiffened that he could not enjoy fly fishing. He asked Simonton if the methods he had been taught for his cancer could also work to reduce calcium deposits and ease the pain in his wrists. Not knowing if it was true, Dr. Simonton assured him that it would certainly work. Several months later, the man called back to thank Simonton. He told him that it was a great pleasure to be pain-free, and that the renewed ability to fish made his retirement a great pleasure.

Months passed, and he called again. He apologized for bothering the doctor, but he did have a question. He had been impotent for a number of years. Maybe the doctor could suggest a way to use what he had learned to overcome this problem as well? Simonton gave him similar ideas in his firmest medical voice. The story had a happy ending: a very pleased patient and a more cheerful spouse as well.

Another well documented case also concerns a man with terminal cancer. A new chemical was available, but only in experimental doses. The patient heard about it and begged his doctor to use it. Treatment was started and the results were remarkable. Each injection reduced the tumor, his overall vitality improved, and his spirits soared. He was deeply grateful to his doctor and to the new treatment. Then a national story appeared about the chemical stating that it was worthless, even a fraud. The patient read the story and within days regressed; the tumor enlarged and his other vital signs declined. His physician thought long and hard about what to do. He went to him and told him that while the first chemical had been a failure, he himself had talked with the discoverer. The problem of potency had been overcome. A new "super" version of the chemical was being air-freighted to the hospital. Tomorrow they would begin daily injections of the superior version. The "new" chemical was duly injected. Almost instantly the patient resumed his rapid and dramatic recovery. What was the role of suggestion in this case? The second chemical, the "super-drug," was pure saline solution, nothing more. The cure arose from the patient's capacity to use self-suggestion effectively to control his own mind and body.

Suggestion, putting ideas into our mind, is one of the tools we have learn to use to support our health, work, and relationships. Understanding how to use the power of suggestion gives you a basic tool which becomes the carrier with which you reinforce intentions most effectively.

What we can conclude is that the mind is the only tool we have to see the world as it is. Not only does it observe, but it also creates the world in which we live. By seeing the role of our own beliefs more clearly, we give ourselves the ability to remold those parts of ourselves which are necessary to bring into reality the future we desire. The limits to this mental work are unknown, but we know that exceeding our past limits is as normal and as natural for people as it is for a tree to grow higher with each new Spring. There is clearly more to the mind than we have uncovered. We will now describe levels of mental capacity which clarify and illuminate some of the unusual facets of our experience.

IV

HIGHER MIND

CONSCIOUS AND SUBCONSCIOUS

The alert conscious mind is in touch with the external world. Through it runs a constant flow of sensations, images, thoughts, feelings, desires, and impulses, as well as observations and analyses of the world around us. Our subconscious mind is a storehouse of memories and the home of fundamental drives that organize our experiences. These ordinary mental activities in turn are sorted and edited before they are either stored or brought into conscious awareness. The subconscious holds the vast bulk of information that we learn throughout our lives. It also contains our repressed childhood memories which may be the birthplace of adult negative habit patterns as well as potential phobias, obsessions, and compulsions.

Freud developed this model of conscious/subconscious so that he might better understand mental illness. As he understood more, he was able to treat his patients more effectively. His discovery that there were subconscious links between apparently unrelated conscious thoughts has been a key to many subsequent discoveries of and elaborations on mental structures. Freud's work, while roundly attacked at the time and still controversial, has been so incorporated into our thinking that most of us assume the reality of a personal subconscious.

Freud's theories do not fully consider the workings of the extremely healthy, creative mind. As a practicing physician he was most interested in reducing mental illness. Freud demonstrated that physical and psychological disturbances were linked to impulses, drives, and fantasies which originated in the subconscious. He found that many mental behaviors including dreams, fantasies, forgetfulness, and mistakes were produced by the same mechanisms that produced mental illness. He helped unravel the tangles of the disturbed, disordered mind, although he and those who followed him only barely investigated the links between intuition or illumination and normal consciousness.

The whole area of "healthy-mindedness" has been unfortunately neglected in modern psychology until recently. There is little guidance in mainstream psychology to help us understand the mental processes of gifted, talented, creative, or spiritually developed individuals.

It appears that Freud's early model of the mind was not only inaccurate, but it was also incomplete. Understanding the subconscious has improved our knowledge of pathology, and understanding the conscious has improved our knowledge of day-to-day thought processes. We still need to examine a higher aspect of consciousness, a creative awareness, that seems to use conscious and subconscious processes. While there are many names for this part of the mind, we will call it the Higher Self, or the Transpersonal, meaning over or above normal consciousness, over and above the constraints of the conscious personality.

WILL AND SYNTHESIS

The Italian psychiatrist Roberto Assagioli saw a need to go beyond Freud's work to fully understand higher mental processes. While he praised psychoanalysis for probing parts of the mind, he saw that it did not adequately explain the higher levels of mental integration present in gifted individuals throughout history. Assagioli concluded that there must be additional parts of the mind; something more than the conscious and the subconscious that were then understood.

He called his work **psychosynthesis**, and suggested that the goal of psychological integration was more than analysis and that this integration should include the entire mind. Assagioli saw individuals "in constant development, growing, actualizing many latent potentialities". Assagioli reasoned that the will is "an essential function of the self and the necessary source or origin of all choices, decisions, and engagements. Therefore, psychosynthesis includes a careful analysis of the various phases of the will such as **deliberation, motivation, decision, affirmation, persistence,** and **execution**. It makes much use of various techniques for arousing, developing, strengthening, and rightly directing the will."

Due to the importance of the will, Assagioli advocated utilizing active techniques to encourage personal growth. He suggested techniques which could aid in:

a. The transformation, sublimation, and direction of psychological energies.

b. The strengthening and maturing of weak or undeveloped functions.

c. The activation of superconscious energies and the rousing of latent potentialities.

Assagioli thus set these positive values on a sound psychological footing by replacing blind faith with technique, and wishful thinking with clinical research. His overall goal was "the conscious and **planned** reconstruction or re-creation of the personality." A person should not be merely content to eliminate neurotic patterns, but he or she should also encourage "the elements and functions coming from the superconscious, such as aesthetic, ethical, religious experience, intuition, and states of mystical consciousness." These he said are "**factual**; are real in the pragmatic sense ... because they are **effective** in producing changes both in the inner and outer worlds." He observed that to change our inner being, we need to plan the changes we desire, to actively participate in creating those changes, and to develop and utilize, not only our lower nature, but also our higher mental powers.

It is from the higher self, Assagioli observed, that "we receive our higher intuition and inspirations — artistic, philosophic or scientific, ethical 'imperatives', and urges to humanitarian and heroic action. It is the source of the higher feelings, such as altruistic love, of genius, and of the states of contemplation, illumination, and ecstasy."

A well-known American psychologist, Carl Rogers, reinforced Assagioli's views. Writing about the attributes of the "fully functioning person", Rogers observed that if one could only establish a situation in which a person felt safe enough, "the wisdom of the organism" would manifest itself. If people in therapy felt safe, they could and would direct their own recoveries. Thus one role of the therapist, in Rogers' thinking, was to allow the higher self to exert its influence. "This newer approach relies more heavily on the individual drive towards growth, health and adjustment. [Therapy] is a matter of freeing [the client] for normal growth and development."

SELF-ACTUALIZATION

Abraham Maslow amplifies Rogers' position with his own observations. His analysis led him to a list of conclusions which he called a "new conception of human sickness and health" which are in sharp contrast to the more limited and pessimistic Freudian view. Maslow concluded that:

1. We have, each of us, an essential inner nature, which is to some degree, natural, intrinsic, given, and in a certain sense, unchangeable or, at least, unchanging.

2. Our inner nature is in part unique and in part species-wide or universal.

3. It is possible to study this inner nature scientifically and to discover, not invent, what it is like.

4. This inner nature, as much as we know of it so far, does not seem to be intrinsically evil, but rather neutral or positively "good." What we call "evil" appears most often to be a secondary reaction to frustration of this intrinsic nature.

5. Since this inner nature is good rather than bad, it is better to bring it out and encourage it than to suppress it. If it is permitted to guide our life, we grow healthy, fruitful, and happy.

6. If this central core is denied or suppressed, we get sick, sometimes in obvious ways, sometimes in subtle ways, sometimes immediately, sometimes later.

7. This inner nature is not strong and overpowering and is unmistakably like the instincts of animals. It is delicate and subtle and easily overcome by **habit, cultural pressure, or wrong attitudes towards it.**

8. Even though delicate, this inner nature never disappears in the normal person — perhaps not even in the sick person. Though denied, it persists underground, forever pressing for actualization.

THE HIGHER SELF

Our inner nature can be stifled, but not destroyed. Whenever we begin to open ourselves up to this inner nature, it unfolds and strengthens. The more we become in touch with our higher or transpersonal self, the more we enter a larger world of expression. We move towards living what Carl Rogers calls "the good life." It is not passivity, not a resting place, nor a lessening of activity. "The good life," says Rogers, "from the point of view of my experience, is the **process of movement** in a direction which the human organism selects when it is inwardly free to move in any direction." Observations of healthy, successful people parallel Rogers' observations of clients in therapy who are in good contact with their higher self. Rogers lists the important characteristics:

An increasing openness to experience

"[It is] a movement away from the pole of defensiveness toward the pole of openness to experience. The individual is becoming more able to listen to himself, to experience what is going on within himself. He is free to live his feelings, subjectively, as they exist and to be freely aware of these feelings."

An increasing tendency to live fully in each moment

"Such living in the moment means an absence of rigidity, of tight organization, of the imposition of structure on experience. It means instead a maximum of adaptability ..."

An increasing trust in one's whole self

Individuals "discover to an ever-increasing degree that if they are open to their experience, doing what 'feels right' proves to be a competent and trustworthy guide to behavior which is truly satisfactory." People are no longer caught in their past perceptions but "permit their total organism...to consider each stimulus, its relative intensity and importance." They no longer rely on memories and previous experiences which confuse and cloud the present moment. One does not become infallible, but one "would always give the best possible answer for the available data. ... any errors, any following of behavior which was not satisfying, would be corrected."

Being creative

A person living the good life is naturally creative. He or she "would not necessarily be 'adjusted' to their culture and would almost certainly not be conformist. Such a person would, I believe, be recognized by a student of evolution as the type most likely to adapt and survive under changing environmental conditions."

More trusting of self and others

"The basic nature of the human being, when flowing freely is constructive and trustworthy ... I have little sympathy with the rather prevalent concept that man is basically irrational, and that his impulses, if not controlled, will lead to destruction of others and self. Man's behavior is exquisitely rational, moving with subtle and ordered complexity towards the goals the organism is endeavoring to achieve."

Life is richer and more satisfying

"I believe it will have become evident why, for me, adjectives such as happy, contented, blissful, enjoyable, do not seem quite appropriate to any general description of this process I have called the good life, even though the person in this process would experience each one of these feelings at appropriate times. The adjectives which seem more generally fitting are adjectives such as enriching, exciting, rewarding, challenging, and meaningful.

This process of the good life is not, I am convinced, a life for the faint-hearted. It involves stretching and growing, of becoming more and more aware of one's potentialities."

THE HIGHER SELF IN ACTION

Assagioli, Maslow, and Rogers described how we function when we are attuned to the capacities of the higher part of our mind. Yet their descriptions were abstract. What does it look like to act from this center?

Here is the famous German composer Mozart writing to a friend:

"When I am, as it were, completely myself, entirely alone and of good cheer ... it is on such occasions that my ideas flow best and most abundantly. Whence and how they come I know not ... All this fires my soul and, provided I am not disturbed, my subject enlarges itself, becomes methodised and defined, on the whole, though it be long, it stands almost complete and finished in my mind, so I can survey it, like a fine picture or a beautiful statue, at a glance. Nor do I hear in my imagination, the parts successively, but I hear them all at once."

Another German composer, Wagner, wrote that the ideas for his music arrived "like a flash of light in the greatest clarity and definiteness, but not altogether in complete detail." The French composer, Saint-Saens, said it most simply when he maintained that in order to compose, one had only to listen. In Beethoven's words, "The new and the original is born without one's thinking of it." These composers understood and used this higher part of the mind; they learned to listen to it and to work from that higher vantage point.

In authors we find the parallel descriptions of the allowing and encouraging of their higher awareness. The Englishman, Charles Dickens, referring to his abilities in prose, stated "Some beneficent power showed it all to me." The novelist Thackery commented, "I have been surprised at the observation made by some of my characters. It seems as if an occult power was moving my pen."

Ideas emerge from what Oliver Wendell Holmes called the "underground workshop of thought." Here is how the English philosopher Bertrand Russell approached his work. "My own belief is that a conscious thought may be planted in the subconscious [higher self] if a sufficient amount of vigor and intensity is put into it ... I have found, for example, that if I have to write upon some rather difficult topic, the best plan is to think about it with very great intensity — the greatest intensity of which I am capable — for a few hours or days, and at the end of that time give orders so to speak that the work is to proceed underground. After some months I return consciously to the topic and find that the work has been done."

My research has found that this kind of success depends on two factors **beyond** pure intention and proper orientation. The first is that the bare necessities, the skills, must be in the subconsciousness. People do not become composers who cannot play a musical instrument, no matter how pure their hearts or how strong their intentions. The second important factor is that this higher mind, the clear, bright, shining, creative, wise part of our selves is a servant, not a master. It is a servant to conscious awareness and to the level of self-concept that we maintain. We achieve only up to the level of our self-concept.

In my geometry class in high school, almost everyone cheated. The reasons are complex, but it was a full-participation, class-wide effort. Our grades could have all been "A's". We were not graded on a curve but on the absolute scores of our tests. To my dumbfounded amazement, the students who normally did A work in other classes got an A in geometry, the students who were B students handed in B work and so on down to a student who, when faced with all the correct answers, almost failed the course. Self-concept was the filter through which the answers flowed; and it was this internal governor that modulated the level of success.

It is important to recall that, as we learn to correctly use our higher faculties, the results will ultimately depend on our progress with our basic goals. The fundamental pace of the higher self is set by the level of personal integrity and self-concept. With this clarification, let us consider some additional levels of functioning of the higher self. As we look over more unusual events, they raise new questions about the power and extent of the human mind.

OTHER FACETS OF THE HIGHER SELF

The Higher Self sometimes communicates through dreams. For example, for several days the scientist Louis Agassiz tried to classify an obscure fossil fish from the parts exposed in a stone slab in which it was embedded. One night he awakened, having dreamed of seeing the fish with all its missing features restored. He returned to his laboratory to see if his vision would help his work. The fossil remained as obscure as ever. The next night, he dreamed again of seeing the fish, but on awakening the images left his mind. Hopeful for a third occurrence, he put a pad and pencil beside his bed. His wife reported "Toward morning the fish reappeared in his dream, with such distinctness that he no longer had any doubt as to its zoological character. Still dreaming, in perfect darkness, he traced these characters on a sheet of paper at his bedside."

"In the morning he was surprised to see, in his nocturnal sketch, features which he thought it was impossible the fossil itself would reveal. He hastened to the Jardin des Plants and, with his drawing as a guide, succeeded in chiseling away the surface of the stone under which portions of the fish proved to be hidden. When wholly exposed, the fossil corresponded with his dream and his drawing, and he succeeded in classifying it with ease."

Other scientists who found answers to problems in dreams include James Watt who solved the problem of casting lead shot after seeing tiny lead balls raining about him in his dream. Elias Howe dreamed the solution to the position of the needle in the first sewing machine. There are hundreds of examples of solutions appearing when the conscious mind is asleep.

A different kind of dream solution suggests that the mind has a still wider scope. After the death of the poet Dante, several concluding verses of his **Paradiso** could not be found. After every plausible place had been searched, his sons decided to write lines to complete the manuscript. Jacopo, one of his sons, then had a dream in which his father appeared and led him to a bedroom in another house. He touched a wall and told his son, "what you have sought for so much is there." With witnesses in tow, Jacopo went to the house and to the room in question. In the wall, in a small niche hidden by a frame, were the lost final verses.

In the hundreds of cases I have observed it is evident that, properly attuned, we gain remarkable advantages using the total mind directly and with clear intention. These examples are not rare, exotic events beyond the reach of most of us. Quite the opposite.

Consider your own life. Have you ever had a dream which foretold a future event? Over half the population of the U.S. report that they have. Have you ever thought about someone you had not seen in months or years, and the phone rings and you hear his or her voice? Have you even thought about distant friends only to have a letter arrive from them that day? It happens more often than we notice.

If you doubt these abilities, raise the question with a group of friends. I recall testing out this idea with a group of first year graduate students in Psychology at Stanford. A more tight-minded, rational, sensible, and gifted group would be hard to find. After an initial wave of "that's all nonsense," I told a few personal stories to indicate what I meant. One after another students recalled similar events in their own lives or in the lives of their parents or grandparents. After the storytelling had gone around the room, I asked why they had all initially called it nonsense. Several students acknowledged that they believed their own experiences but had never felt free to share them with others because they were afraid of being mocked.

SELF-CONCEPT AND THE HIGHER SELF

It is a well kept secret that we all have an active, functional, and operational higher mind. It is a delight to acknowledge this aspect of ourselves, and to learn how to use it more effectively. This higher mind has a vast capacity for solving problems, a capacity so well developed and so accurate that, when we first understand and appreciate it, we wonder why our lives have not been more fruitful. We need to understand why this flawless problem-solving, creative thrust of consciousness does not always make life as easy as it could be.

What emerges is a strange but powerful truth. This accurate, even inspired, part of the mind is without goals, without intention, and without any agenda of its own. It does not strive, it does not worry, it does not doubt, and it does not glory in its own success.

The willingness of the personality to be successful is limited and controlled by the level of self-concept. In case after case, when people are motivated to resolve a problem, the quality of their solution is **predetermined** by their opinion of their own abilities. Solutions are a direct reflection of our initial attitude. When we speak of ourselves as our own "worst enemy," we are describing the restriction our consciousness places on our higher powers. A man once told me that he knew his higher self was asleep on the job. I asked why. "Because of the string of bad investments I've made over the years." He rolled off a list of investment disasters to illustrate that no matter how he invested, it would turn sour, and he would lose money. His luck was so consistently poor in fact, that it was remarkable. I asked him more about himself. He spoke of his capacity to solve problems at work, how he had advanced himself through hard work and long hours. He had come from a poor background. He was a self-made man and proud of it. I asked him about his investments. He said, "I can never make a good investment, never!" I was startled because he said it in the same tone, the same powerful, forceful, prideful manner in which he reported his accomplishments. It was clear that his problem-solving capacity was not asleep, but that the problem that his conscious mind had assigned this same capacity was to find investments **which would not work**. His self-concept maintained that he was a person who would gain money only through deliberate work. Thus, his long string of losing investments was an inspired solution to the problem of maintaining his identity.

We do not get what we wish, but what we think we deserve. The mind is the bond servant of our self-concept. If your self-concept is low, then opportunities for pleasure, success, and advancement will be deliberately overlooked. If you have a high self-concept, opportunities are noticed, grasped, and developed.

This linkage between two portions of the mind helps explain the life changes, the career advancements, and the seemingly lucky incidents that graduates of Omega and similar seminars report. It also clarifies why so many good books and courses which present how to use higher consciousness do not produce consistently good results. Without self-concept development, the powers of the higher conscious are still at the mercy of subconscious habit patterns.

William James, in his book **The Varieties of Religious**

77

Experience, examines spiritual and religious experiences including the neurotic behavior of saints. What he observed was that individuals, even those with saintly attributes, behaved poorly at times; rudely, stupidly, selfishly, dishonestly. James searched for an explanation for the coexistence of their virtues with their evident vices. He concluded that we have many selves; many compartments of identity. Each identification has a cluster of habits associated with it. He believed that if we do not pick one of these and hold fast to it, our behavior drifts from habit cluster to habit cluster, determined more by outside forces than by our own will. He thought that we should pick one central identity, one that we would like to strengthen and consolidate it by willpower and conscious effort. While I have not had the opportunity to work with saints, I have found that James' descriptions parallel my experiences.

A better understanding of the approaches to successful problem solving can help achieve personal goals, provided, that the basic work, improving self-concept, has begun.

V

PROBLEM SOLVING

*To know
rather consists of opening out a way
whence the imprisoned splendor may escape
than in effecting entry for a light
supposed to be without.*
Robert Browning

You are already a superb problem solver. What you might lack is experience, practice, or well developed skills. While children are natural problem solvers, adults sometimes need help in reconnecting with their basic capacities and overcoming the blocks that prevent full use of all parts of the mind.

The pivotal way in which we block ourselves is by believing that we are uncreative. This, as we know, is a problem of self-concept. When this self-concept limit is overcome, we can explore specific information and skills which can improve our problem solving.

First class problem solvers are aware of the walls that seem to spring up between them and potential solutions. Many of these obstacles are obvious, but noticing them and overcoming them is a master skill which improves as we develop. As our self-concept rises, we seek out more problems, take on more creative projects, and investigate new avenues of self-expression. Each new arena presents new problems, but also exposes new obstacles. Each of us has inner habits which can restrict the free flow of our creative energy.

Understanding these inner blocks helps even the most skilled and successful artists, inventors, and proficient problem solvers. What are some of the most troublesome emotional, cultural, environmental, intellectual, and perceptual blocks? We shall review examples of each. As you read over the description, see if you can recall times or situations when you were aware of each particular block. If you prefer, recall examples from your family or friends. In this way you will become more sensitive not only to these blocks within yourself, but in others as well. The first step on the road to change is recognition.

EMOTIONAL BLOCKS

Emotional blocks are feelings that interfere with your willingness or your capacity to solve problems. They appear in many forms, a few of which we shall consider.

Lack of challenge

Sometimes a problem appears to be too simple, too easy, or too obvious to hold your attention. It is a problem beneath your intelligence or your job; it's a task which should be delegated, put aside, and let slide. It is a job "anyone could do."

For example, I need to restructure my files about this book which have grown unwieldy. It is not a difficult task, but it is cumbersome. To do so I must make a series of small decisions, none of which interest me. I put it off because more interesting problems are forever presenting themselves. The result is that the original task is not completed. Another time I needed a small brass fixture for an item which had broken at home. I knew that I would need to call around for the part, disassemble the object, check the new part to be sure that it fit and reassemble it. The time it took to do the task (when I actually did it) was under thirty minutes, including the calls and the drive to the store. The time to get over my lack of interest, however, was almost three months.

We are continually accumulating these kinds of problems. To learn how to be willing to solve them is the challenge! It was said of Brother Lawrence, author of the medieval classic, **The Practice of the Presence of God**, that although he never hurried and never worked quickly, he did twice as much work as any other person in the monastery. Doing what needs to be done is a gift and a skill.

Need for quick answers

If you observe problem-solving groups, you will often notice one member who comes up with a solution almost immediately. Once a person like this finds a solution to a problem, he or she locks onto it and won't let go. Since a solution has been found, they say, the group should begin to implement it rather than continue to consider alternatives.

I used to admire that attitude. Here were people who leapt over the problem and had a solution before I even understood the problem. However, what I have learned is that the very speed of their solution finding is a clue to their emotional block — fear. The problem itself is disturbing to them. These people are uncomfortable in a world with unsolved problems; problems that create doubts and an unclear future. They seek, therefore, not a good solution, but any solution which can diminish their anxiety. Fleeing from fear, from uncertainty, obscures any determined examination of other, more considered solutions; it also precludes looking for the best solution.

What on the surface looks like quick-wittedness, followed by impatience, is actually a lack of confidence. When you settle for patch jobs, quick fixes, or temporary solutions, your need to stop rather than solve the problem prevents finding better, or more substantial solutions.

Fear of making a mistake

Fear of making mistakes is probably the most common stumbling block. When you do nothing, wait for someone else to take responsibility, or allow your ideas to be superseded, you lower the possibility that **you** will make a mistake (and reduce your fear). You also lower your chances (to zero) of finding a solution of which you can be proud. One definition of life is that it is a process of making mistakes, learning, and making new mistakes. This is not a cynical idea but a cheerful one. Problem solvers, inventors, creators, and artists make far more mistakes than an average person and take more risks as well. One common theme that recurs in the lives of creative people is their willingness to take risks in their work and in their personal lives.

The following are rules of thumb for risk-takers:
1. If more than half of your ideas work the first time, your work is not very inventive.
2. If everything you do works, you are taking no risks at all.
3. If everything you invent fails, you are not learning from your mistakes.

One final examination I gave took place on Lake Lagunita

at Stanford University. One year, the task was to design, construct, and operate a vessel that would hold four students, cost no more than $30.00, and be able to go out to the middle of the lake on one face, then turn over and come back on a different face — safely. In addition to grades, there were two awards: one for the fastest vehicle to complete the course, the other for the most innovative vehicle. The final was well attended; 500 spectators, one local television news crew, girl and boy friends, rooting parties, bystanders, and the class members. Any failure would be extremely visible. The exam, run as a race, was exciting and close.

The winning entry was a teardrop shaped container built by a team with excellent mathematical skills as well as nautical experience and who had trained in their craft for a week preceding the final. The winning innovative craft was an open oval shaped like a ring with a twist in it. It was a Mobius strip, a construction which seems to have only one side. I had seen them made from a strip of paper as a curiosity; but had never seen one built to hold four excited graduate students. They paddled out to the middle of the lake, turned it "inside out" and began their return. Twenty yards from shore the frame broke and began to sink. Furious paddling moved it closer to shore but it went under before it finished. The design was brilliant, but it was not welded properly; the stress of the race literally tore it apart. "How do you feel about your craft falling apart?" I asked. They told me that none of them had even been sure that it would make it to the center of the lake. They had decided to take a real risk.

It is to the bold that the rewards belong. Take no risks — get no rewards. Real risk taking assumes a self-concept which takes failures in stride and enjoys the successes. Most inventions do not work the first or the tenth time; each failure is a step on the way. Those who stop with the initial failures never taste the sweetness of eventual completion.

83

Desire for order

A close cousin to the fear of risk-taking is the desire for order. The need for order is a sensible part of any large organization but it becomes an obstacle when the need for order overwhelms the need for creative responses. Problems are exactly those issues that don't fit into any previous order. People who thrive on order squash problems with rule books, manuals, and regulations. The problems remain but they go underground.

Have you ever been told that such and such "is not covered in the regulations." What you are being told is that your problem is one that has not already been solved and you should therefore go away. When faced with this block, I have found that a direct appeal to a person's higher mind sometimes helps. I look at the person and say, "this is your special area, you understand it, and I don't. What would you do to solve this problem?" If they become reflective, you can relax — their problem-solving faculties are coming into play and they will search for a solution. If they reply as before, "It's not in the regulations," ask for their supervisor, or anybody else, and try for the higher mind again.

At one point in college I saw that I would have great difficulty fulfilling a set of requirements before graduation. I went to the appropriate office and laid out the problem. The woman helping me studied it every which way. She agreed with me that there seemed to be no solution that would not cost me a lot of time and energy. In desperation I inquired, "Can you think of another way?" She frowned and then, just for an instant, she asked herself for a solution. Her face cleared; she laughed to herself and turned back to me. "There is a solution ... take the classes you wish, then come back to us six weeks before graduation. We will look it over, recognize that there can be no way to change anything, make an exception in your case, and you will graduate. Just one favor, when you come back, don't tell this office where you got the idea."

There are always solutions — not always comfortable or easy solutions — but every problem has alternative paths. If we truly wish to be free of problems, then we are wishing to live like a rock in a subterranean cave — no problems, no opportunities, no life.

Judgment, not creativity

Preferring to judge ideas rather than create them is a subtle block, often misperceived as a virtue by management and administration. People burdened with this block may be highly placed and highly paid, even if not highly appreciated.

Can you recall a time when a group was struggling to solve a problem; anything from how to position a new product to where to hold a charity auction? As ideas were raised, one member of the group continually ferreted out flaws in everyone's ideas.

"We tried that three years ago and it cost us a bundle."

"You haven't taken into account the parking problems."

"We can't afford to hire anyone extra now to fill that position."

"That vendor might help, but he's having delivery problems of his own."

These are examples of "YES, BUT ... YES, BUT ..." These people, with their wisdom and their experience, are "idea-snuffers." They are so able and determined to see the defects in an idea that they rarely allow an idea to mature. If you observe them carefully, these are people who are afraid, afraid not only of making mistakes themselves, but afraid to let others make mistakes. By focusing early, closely, and tightly on the defects in an idea, they prevent an initial proposal from evolving through a normal pattern of testing, modification, and improvement. Their premature criticism not only restricts potential for failure, but limits success as well.

It is easier to be a judge, a critic, or an editor than to be a creator, an artist, a writer, or an inventor. Every idea is born with rough edges, wrapped in false starts, and peppered with mistaken assumptions. Almost any idea can be belittled in its first stages; conversely, almost any idea can improve if people are encouraged to support it.

What happens to a group with an idea-snuffer in it? At first ideas flow, but gradually the production of new ideas slows until it ceases entirely. The idea-snuffer bullies the part of us that is afraid to feel foolish and is embarrassed when it makes mistakes. If every time we come up with an idea we feel foolish, we soon learn that it is easier and less threatening to have no ideas than to have poorly received ones.

There is nothing wrong with critical judgment — if you can control it. It is said that a writer has two conflicting forces within him: a creator and a critic. If the creator is too strong, what is written is trash. If the critic is too strong, nothing gets written at all. A proper inner balance develops fine writing. Individual writers achieve this balance in their own way. Anthony Trollope wrote quickly, carefully, and methodically and rewrote very little. Leo Tolstoy rewrote endlessly, writing each of his novels as many as seven times before letting it out of his hands. Even then, he rewrote his proof sheets as heavily as he had revised the manuscripts.

Each of us knows the feeling of having an idea primed and ready to share when an inner voice says, "Wait. This idea will sound crazy. Hold it. Reconsider." The inner battle begins; sometimes the creator wins; at other times the critic pushes the idea away and you say or do nothing.

Highly creative people burst with ideas. They know that the capacity to develop ideas is essential for their continued success. Often my engineering students worry about something they have invented for a class assignment. They worry about losing the potential patent rights to the industrial sponsor or to the university. I ask them to evaluate their thinking process, as well

86

as the individual product.

Is this going to be your last good idea?

If so, protect it by all means.

If not, enjoy the pleasure of creating.

Creative people are like fishermen; they all have stories of the big one that got away. Creative people are skilled fishermen; they catch a big one now and then. A friend of mine invented a product for a new company. The prototype failed at a crucial demonstration. The idea was good, but the company never recovered. What did he do? He literally went next door to another small start-up, worked on their new product, became their chief scientist, and aided them into the marketplace with a product that was a stunning success.

Fear is at the core of all emotional blocks. Wrapped around that core are repressed and recalled memories of being judged and found lacking, inner doubts about your own originality. As those doubts lessen in intensity, the emotional blocks lift, more ideas become conscious, and your creativity is enhanced.

CULTURAL BLOCKS

Preserving the Status Quo

Every culture strives for stability, predictability, and order. We find safety in a world that is regular, that runs this year the way it did last year. In a Peanuts cartoon, Linus weeps and wails about the disappearance of the snow. Lucy tells him it will come back next year. "You mean, winter comes back? I thought it was gone forever." We need a certain amount of stability, but too much continuity becomes a restriction. Consider these statements, said in business meetings of clients. Each one prevents a new idea, method, or approach from being tried:

"We've always done it this way."

"That needs to be reviewed by higher management."

"That's not our department."

"It's not in the budget."

"It's not in the budget" is one of the finest idea-killers available to unenlightened management. By definition, **new** ideas cannot be in the budget. One test I use to determine the health of a company is to observe how ideas not-in-the-budget are incorporated into ongoing operations. Tom Peters, in researching his book **In Pursuit of Excellence**, found that innovative products came from "the wrong people with the wrong backgrounds in the wrong department in the wrong division at the wrong time." This was true of almost every case in the most successful companies.

"Don't be foolish" or "That's not logical."

Those responses to an idea may indicate that the idea arises from the higher self. Often such ideas are not logical at their inception. The ideas that are found to be sound only after study and deliberation at first may feel like intruders; like clowns at a formal dinner.

"That's not the way we do things here (in this family, this department, this company)."

Here is another wonderful clue for your own creativity. You cannot originate an idea which is "the way things already are." New ways slash across accepted practices. A software company, for example, put out a product that allows one computer to send "mail" to another. The cost of the product? Ninety-nine cents. How could this be? For ninety-nine cents the buyer gets a disc which runs the program and allows fifteen letters to be sent. The program then stops itself and can not be run again. If the user likes the service, the full package is available at full price. That wasn't the way things were done in the software industry. Its an industry which prides itself on innovation, but which already has a culture replete with rules, methods, models, and normal ways of doing business. For creative people, being told "That's not the way we do it around here" gets them excited, as aroused as a bull in the arena seeing a red cape. The challenge delights them; it is a new opportunity, a new fence to go around, push down, or jump over.

Cultural taboos

Another kind of cultural limit is the taboo. Every close-knit group has social rules as certain things are simply not done. For example, there is a universal taboo in all known cultures against incest. There are taboos in many cultures against marrying your second cousin. There are taboos in some social groups against swearing. There are taboos in some companies about certain kinds of clothes. There are taboos about what can be said on radio, on television, in films, in books. Each different set of cultural restrictions is well understood by the members of that group. New members make mistakes that are unthinkable to those who are long-term residents.

When San Francisco became home to many Asian refugees after the Vietnam war, some trapped the birds, squirrels, and other wild animals in the city parks. They had no taboo against killing and eating these animals. They were amazed to find out that it was not an acceptable practice. It never entered their minds that it might be taboo to hunt animals in the parks.

We all have inner limitations; areas of our awareness that we avoid. We maintain these inner taboos to protect ourselves from inner pain, from difficult memories, from shameful experiences, from recalling our own weaknesses. While these restrictions may protect us from uncomfortable moments, the taboo extracts a heavy price. Any area of our mind which we cannot visit cannot be used. The more creative we allow ourselves to become, the more areas we restore to serve us.

I once gave a talk to a funeral society. It was a non-profit group that helped people plan ahead to reduce unnecessary expenses and trauma for bereaved families. I elected to give a cheerful talk, highlighting the incongruities in our culture about death and our fear of **actually** dying (People don't die, they "pass away"). It was well received by most of the group but several people were offended. They said that it was wrong, wrong, wrong, to make light of anything linked to death. One woman taped the talk and later played it for her eighty-year-old mother. Afterwards, they had their first real talk about aging and death. The mother was able to unburden herself about her own illness and to share her fears of dying. Understanding that a taboo area is a dangerous area of the mind does not make it off-limits. It is a potential storehouse of energy and possible new ideas.

We all benefit from living in a stable culture, but we also need to be able to recognize that the limits of that culture are arbitrary. At times, we need to be able to transcend those limits should a situation demand it. "But that's impossible," says Alice to the Red Queen in **Alice Through the Looking Glass**. "My dear," the Queen responds, "I believe in two impossible things before breakfast." The Queen's diet was her way to stay flexible. Well digested, it leads to considering no problem as unsolvable. Take the case of the Wright brothers. They knew full well that both culture and conventional science believed that powered flight was against natural law. In fact, the United States Patent Office had turned down earlier patent applications, stating that heavier-than-air flight was impossible. Until it was accomplished, it was indeed impossible. Impossible may be only in the eye of the beholder.

A creative person tests out taboo areas, as a skater tests the ice at the edge of a frozen lake. If it actually is thick enough, the skater glides right past the "NO SKATING, THIN ICE" signs and enjoys the whole lake.

ENVIRONMENTAL BLOCKS

Your creative potential can be lessened by a difficult or hostile environment. You are most free when you work in an atmosphere which supports your freedom. Let us consider some external conditions that can diminish or restrict creativity.

Job insecurity

Your job may be insecure for very valid, external reasons. Your department, your company, your whole industry might be shaky. Business may be poor. New competition may crowd your company's goods or services out of the market. The union may have won demands that make your job unprofitable for the company. You may see that your supervisor doesn't encourage promotion. You may be in an area in which there is high turn-over. Dozens of real reasons exist for job insecurity, and the net effect of insecurity is anxiety. While anxious, most people are less creative. Our most basic needs are security and safety. When those are missing, we become cautious and defensive. We are more liable to go by the book than to strive for improvements or seek out innovations.

Making your job more secure can be a problem in and of itself. You are not at fault if you find your creativity thwarted by job uncertainties. However, you can turn your energies toward creating a more stable, more supportive job environment for yourself.

Closed-minded management

There are cases (far too many) of people in supervisory jobs who imagine that their task is to think, while those who report to them should merely carry out their commands. For example, a man involved in marketing technical products tells of a meeting held by his supervisor's boss to consider what they could do to reverse a serious sales decline. "He called the meeting, he said, 'to get our ideas, and opinions'. However, in the two hours, he talked almost non-stop. When others began to speak, he cut them off. He allowed no ideas other than his own and **it was his ideas that had led us into the problem**." What were the results of the meeting? "I was angry and frustrated. Now, I'm thinking of leaving the company." The man was talented, creative, and has a zest for life. What he concluded, from that meeting, was that his own creativity was neither asked for, desired, nor even considered. He began to look for alternatives to his situation. He enrolled in some classes, improved his skills, and soon left to work for another company.

Lack of support for new ideas

The authors of **In Search of Excellence** describe "product champions." These are people who envision a new idea, development, or product, and fight for it inside the company. Many companies encourage these champions. Other companies shy away from giving such individuals room to exceed their job responsibilities. These companies may accept new ideas, but they are less likely to keep their most creative people.

A champion usually needs high self-assurance to overcome the lassitude usual in even the most supportive companies. A case in point occurred in the corporate headquarters of a major insurance company. A technical writer was hired to update a series of specialized manuals for the field offices. The new format had been approved before he was hired. The new writer found that the format itself was outdated — far more than the manuals he was supposed to be rewriting. He spoke with his supervisor who told him that his job did not extend to revising the format. He did not take his supervisor's "no" as a final answer. He spent time on his own roughing out a new format. He showed it to his boss and to his boss's supervisor. Both of them liked it. His job assignment was changed, as was his title, and soon thereafter his pay scale. He pushed against the system to protect and test his own ideas. If he had accepted the early defeat, he could have become disheartened and disappointed which could have been reflected in his later work.

The larger and more formal a company's structure, the more difficult it is for new ideas to find support. Many large corporations are aware of this and deliberately create smaller internal entities to foster creativity. If you have a new idea, see how it is first heard and evaluated. If the initial reaction is favorable, is there a way to move it farther? If the initial reaction is unfavorable, is there another way to go? Finding ways to insure that your ideas flourish is fundamental to maintaining the flow of those ideas.

Lack of trust between people

If you don't trust others, you will not share ideas. If you don't share ideas, you will rarely generate them. Trusting others is related to how much you trust yourself and to the level of trust of those around you. Some situations do not breed trust. A supervisor who feels threatened may create an atmosphere of distrust where none existed before. Distrust blinds people to their desire to help, support, and encourage one another. We do our best when we have friends around us to cheer for us when we do well and to catch us should we falter.

Distractions

Not all environmental blocks are interpersonal. Your physical environment is also important. Does it promote or preclude creativity? Industrial studies have found that when creative people are allowed to design their own work areas, they are concerned with the following, in order of importance:

privacy
extraneous noise

heat, cold, dust, etc.
access to equipment, and other people

Their primary desire is to minimize interruptions. Creative people love to work on problems; they love to work hard, and to work long hours. They play with problems, teasing out aspects missed on the first or second or tenth consideration. To do this they need unbroken blocks of time. Some creative people thrive in groups and prefer to work closely with others. They form creative teams which have the same concerns as creative individuals. The group wants privacy, quiet, etc. Inside the team area, they usually prefer an open space where no one is more than a shout away.

Look at your own work environment. Is it designed to allow you to work creatively? If not, what changes might you make? If you are a manager, what can you do for those who work for you so that their work might be more creative as well? As you observe yourself and your own style, you can more easily establish goals to ensure that your environment supports your own creative style.

INTELLECTUAL BLOCKS

Intellectual blocks limit the proper use of information; restrictions on information restrict solutions.

Incorrect or outdated information

Spotting incorrect or outdated information is extremely difficult when you are in the midst of a task. To determine what is already known is different from making new discoveries. Both are necessary. I once supervised several students who had been asked to design a new way to make changes on a computer screen from a keyboard. They began the task with great gusto and soon came up with a fine idea. They reported their idea to the sponsor. He sent them to a scientist working in the corporation who told them that he had invented their idea four years earlier. They were confused and discouraged, but soon returned to the problem and came up with a second, novel solution. A return trip to the corporation led them to another researcher who was in the process of filing a patent very close to their idea. Gloom precluded creative work for several weeks. I instructed, prodded, cajoled, and consoled and finally, they took the project on again. This time, however, they did a substantial review of research already done. They located a promising area and developed a third original idea. It was indeed a breakthrough and was immediately snapped up by the company for further development.

Limited problem-solving strategies

A limited approach to problems is a key concern for motivated, high self-concept people. We all have our favorite ways of solving problems. We write them down, we sketch them, we tell others our ideas, we build models, we fantasize solutions, we list, and we dream. Each of us has a short list of what works for us. None of us uses all the available strategies any more than we play all available sports. We benefit from learning new strategies and new methods to solve problems.

Here is one method of changing strategies. Below you will find a partial list of problem solving strategies. Pick a problem, and see which methods you would use from this list to solve it. Then try a few methods you would not usually use. See the difference in the variety and quality of your solutions.

Approaches to problems

Clarify
Adapt
Substitute

Generalize
Force
Define
Exaggerate
Diagram
Symbolise
Transform
Incubate
List
Randomize
Work backwards
Classify
Chart

Using the wrong language

It is often difficult for us to grasp that a problem might be better described by a series of drawings or by mathematical formulas than in words. When illustrating this block with companies, I produce a bag in which there is a wooden block cut in odd ways. One edge is triangular; there is a square edge and some other surfaces that each have a chunk taken out of them. Then I ask the best communicator in the company to help me — usually the president or the director of marketing. I ask that person to feel the block inside the bag and then, without looking at it, describe it to those present. I ask the others to draw what they hear, and to come up with a representation of the block.

It is always a struggle. I am asking for a verbal description of a visual form. Most people don't describe shapes well in words and often the descriptions leave the group hopelessly confused. The questions that are asked usually make the situation worse. Several very creative executives, after false starts, came up with ways to convey the information. One asked the listeners to think

96

of it as a geometry problem, then he described each corner. Another successful presenter asked the group to imagine a huge cube of butter and then asked them to slice various bits of it away until this unusual object emerged. Both of these presenters reframed the problem in different languages: one analytic, the other visual.

After the discomfort of this exercise has dissipated, I ask how often people in the company have discussed a change in a part or a drawing or a repair in the field over the phone. It is common, of course, but now the group can see that there is a high risk of failure in using the improper frame for a problem.

Consider a problem — any problem. Do you know whether to use:

A written description?
A series of drawings?
A film or slide presentation?
Audio tapes?
Models or mock-ups?
An interactive computer program?

It depends on the demands of the problem and your own capacities. Familiarity and skill with different languages expands the range of problems that you can enjoy and solve.

PERCEPTUAL BLOCKS

Perceptual blocks are blinders and prevent correct viewing of a problem in the first place. These blocks are powerful, pervasive, and difficult to uncover. Fortunately, they are often easy to see in others, so we can use our abilities to see others' limitations to help us eventually uncover our own.

Seeing what you expect

There is a major variation of perceptual blindness which deserves special consideration. It is the loss of the ability to see freshly, to see with "beginner's eyes." We all experience this as we get used to one point of view, one set of beliefs, or one way of living our lives. A gentle word for this is preconceptions, beliefs we have about a future situation. Here are a few samples:

> "Students are getting lazier every year."
> "You can't trust lawyers."
> "People can always be motivated by more money."
> "It's useless to bring up such-and-such with her. She never listens."
> "I don't have to taste it. I know it's yucky."

We all have some preconceptions. The unkind word for them is prejudices. A prejudice is a belief founded on inadequate knowledge, yet held even when reality contradicts it. We are all familiar with racial prejudice and with stereotyping. Negative habit patterns are also a form of personal prejudice. "I can't ..." prejudges our own capacity to handle a future event. "I can't" is a rigid mental structure that resists reality testing. You will not solve problems if you approach them "knowing" that you can't solve them.

"I haven't yet" describes the past more accurately than "I can't" and avoids perceptual blinding. If you must see what you expect to see, and that is a deep human tendency, then at least consider what inventors and problems solvers expect to see. They look ahead to solving their future problems, or at least to enjoying the opportunity.

What can be done to overcome these blocks to our creative flow? We made them, therefore we can unmake them as well. No one has ever said it better than the comic strip character Pogo:

"We have met the enemy and he is us."

A tendency to limit the problem

We all like to bring a problem down to size. However, shrinking a problem can sometimes prevent us from solving it at

98

all. When we first see a problem, we bring out our best tools and our expertise to work toward a solution. And why not? Why not start with our skills and the bodies of information which we know from our own experience.

There are, in fact, reasons for proceeding more slowly at first, more globally, even more vaguely.

Consider the following problem. A family is in conflict; each member is displeased, upset and angry at the others. How should I work on the problem of understanding what is wrong so that harmony might be re-established? My answer might depend on what kind of expert eyes I turn on this family. If I am a physician, I might look at their physical illnesses. If I am a nutritionist, I might look for dietary imbalances. If I am a psychologist, I might look for neurotic behaviors. If I am a social worker, I might focus on the economic concerns. If I am a relative, I might see patterns that I recall from the previous generation. Each expert may see some aspect of the problem and may be of help. Yet there is a real risk that our expert eyes **predetermine** what we see. Our own expertise is mixed with our wish to be an expert and appear knowledgeable. Also, our expert information may limit what we can see. I have known many people who work for years on problems with one kind of expert only to have the problem resolved in weeks by a different expert whose skills were more appropriate.

The classic version of this restriction is the story of the blind men and the elephant. A group of blind men were led to an enclosure which held an elephant. None of the blind men had ever encountered such a beast. Each one approached it, touched it, and came away. Later they spoke to one another.

"It is like a great stone pillar," said the first.

"Not at all," said the second, "It is like a great sheet of leather."

"Absurd," said a third, "It is like a stiff broom."

The fourth blind man laughed aloud. "How foolish you all are. This beast is smooth, and cool, and hard as marble."

They are probably still arguing. We who can view the whole beast can see that the first was describing the legs, the second the ears, the third the tail, and the last one the tusk. Each perceived the elephant through their own narrow, yet correct, experience.

As a general consultant, I am often asked in after a specialist has been hired, researched, reported, and left. Rarely do I find the specialist inadequate or poorly trained, yet the problem remains. Specialists often are unable to step back from the problem if stepping back places them outside their expertise.

To help correct this block, you might ask yourself:

Is what I see the whole problem?

Would someone else see it differently?

If so, what might they see that I would overlook?

Restating a problem in different ways often casts light on initial blind spots and opens up other solutions.

VI

OVERCOMING BLOCKS

Fortunately, there are more ways to solve problems than there are ways to block solutions. The more ways we know, the more we can use.

Each is, in fact, a world by itself. There are dozens of ways available; this brief introduction is to encourage your own exploration. First we will consider a theory about how we approach reality, then we will turn to more specific ways to approach individual problems.

A FAVORITE WAY OF THINKING

Each of us favors one or more senses in our thinking. For example, some of us use visual tools to approach problems. We image, see, look at, and observe. These graphic visual modes are our normal way of getting started. When someone describes a

101

problem to us, we respond by trying to **see** the problem clearly, to **look** for solutions.

Some of us are more auditory. We listen to a problem, resonate with it, sound it out, and talk it over. These approaches derive from hearing. A third style is tactile, or physical. We push and pull on a problem, bounce it around, or take it apart. We grasp the essentials of a problem and wrestle with it until we force a solution. Problems are treated as if they were physical objects.

Each of us has a preferred style, which is our major way of problem solving. The less preferred modes are less developed and less available to consciousness. Successful problem solvers are able to work in many modes. They are also able to blend approaches, as well as work with people whose dominant style differs from their own.

For example, I am by habit a visualizer. I like to see things illustrated or written out. I take notes, make lists and visualize answers. Over the years I have learned to work more with auditory and tactile approaches to problems. I have illustrated problems through story-telling. I have also learned to use hand tools. I am better able to repair things, and have become more aware of what is going on in my garden. As a result I am less afraid of problems which are not my style. I have been part of teams operating machinery and have coached students in speaking skills; situations I would have avoided earlier.

When you work in a different mode, you are using mind muscles that usually don't come into play. Your mind moves stiffly at first, but it gradually warms up to the new mode. Here is a brief example of how the choice of approach can determine your ability to solve a given problem:

If you take a sheet of paper and fold it over, the folded paper is twice the thickness of a single sheet. If you could keep folding it over and over twenty times, how thick would the piece of paper be?

Method I (tactile): Imagine yourself doing this physically — fold after fold. How thick can you feel the paper getting?

Method II (visual): Visualize it. See a huge sheet of paper being folded getting thicker as it goes. How high can you see the folded sheet getting?

Method III (analytic): Now treat it as a mathematical problem. Let a set of symbols replace the paper. Thickness of paper $= T$. Thickness of paper times $2 = 2$ Thicknesses or $2T$. A third fold would be $2 \times 2T$, a fourth fold $= 2 \times 2 \times 2 \times T$. Twenty folds would be 2 to the twentieth power times T or $2 \times 2 \times 2 \times 2 \times 2 \times 2 \times 2 \times 2 \times 2 \times 2 \times 2 \times 2 \times 2 \times 2 \times 2 \times 2 \times 2 \times 2 \times 2 \times 2$, an astonishingly large number. The folded paper is miles high.

Notice that when you changed strategies, different solutions became plausible. Staying with a physical strategy in this case obscured the problem, a visual approach was no better. Finally a third way of considering the problem led to the solution.

Approaching problems with multiple strategies is one way to get hold of the entire elephant.

Can you discover your own favored strategies?

Can you find ways to extend your range?

ACTIVE PROBLEM SOLVING

Here is a rapid way to expand your flexibility. We tend to link the verb "to solve" with the word "problem." However, the verb by itself doesn't give direction. Let us take the first verb from the list of strategies given in the last chapter, the verb "clarify." By developing some of the ways to clarify, we can begin to see how expansive our capacity to change strategies might become.

Ways to Clarify

By reflection
By illustration and definition
By amplification of inconsistencies
By comparison of similarities
By questioning underlying assumptions
By locating points of difficulty
By questioning meanings of terms
By relating to feelings or behaviors
By summarizing a series of steps
By examining alternatives
By recasting the problem in a different form

Each process can open another doorway. When a solution eludes you, step back a moment. Choose a way to clarify from this list. Return to the problem again, using the new approach. You will find this to be easy and astonishingly useful. Approaching the problem in a new way revitalizes your capacity to discover a solution.

OPENNESS TO EXPERIENCE

Maslow studied self-actualizing people; the healthiest people he could find. He anticipated that they would all be extremely creative. This was not the case. He also studied creative people, assuming that they would be mentally healthy. This was not always the case, either.

However, he reported that healthy people were often creative and that creative people were often healthy. What he found in both groups was an openness to experience. Moreover he discovered a willingness to see reality without the selective filtering of prejudices, preconceptions, negative habit patterns, or previous observations.

"Very frequently, it appeared that an essential aspect of Self-actualizing creativeness was a special kind of perceptiveness that is exemplified by the child in the fable who saw that the Emperor had no clothes on. These people can see the fresh, the raw, the concrete, the ideographic, as well as the generic, the abstract, the rubicized, the categorized and classified. Consequently they live more in the real world of nature than in the verbalized world of concepts, abstractions, expectations, beliefs and stereotypes that most people confuse with the real world ... the creativeness was spontaneous, effortless, innocent, easy, a kind of freedom from stereotypes and cliches".

How can we become more open to experience? By lowering the barriers we erect to protect ourselves on the one hand, and by plunging more deeply into experience on the other. I recall walking in San Francisco with Stewart Brand, the creator of the Whole Earth Catalog, who is also a gifted photographer. He kept exclaiming, "Look at that!" I'd look in the direction he indicated and would see another city street or a tangle of wires or the edge of a building. What was I supposed to be seeing? Stewart would point out the marvelous couple sitting on the curb, the pattern of wires like a musical staff singing with birds, the cornice of a building, its marble scrollwork turned rose colored by the afternoon sun. He showed me what was already there; he was teaching me to see. Realize that others may be able to help you see or hear or taste more vividly. Wine tasting with an expert, listening to music with a musician, going to a rodeo with a cowboy or to a rock concert with your teenager enlarges your world. An enlarged world enriches your problem-solving capacity.

SOLUTIONS FROM ANYWHERE

Be open to the most unlikely possibilities. If you ask creative problem-solvers for their most surprising adventures you will be assaulted with improbable story upon improbable story. For example, a recent Omega graduate wanted a tape recorder. Two days later, in a pile of leaves near his home he found a plastic bag holding just such a tape player and a small calculator. He took them in and showed it to his accountant who said. "Wow, I've been looking for a calculator just like that one for weeks! Can I use it?" Why was that story about problem solving, and not just about luck? There is a large element in luck in the lives of creative people. It is as if they know how to manipulate the world so that more of the luck rolls into their pockets. Each individual has their own special way and they all maintain a high belief in their capacity to be lucky, another aspect of their overall high self-concept.

Here are two more stories which challenged me to re-examine how the world actually does work and to expand my own realm of possibilities.

A woman I know wanted to visit Hong Kong. At a party she met a world-traveling photographer who had just returned from a job in Hong Kong. She asked him questions, and told him how much she wanted to go there sometime. He laughed, and asked if she would be willing to go tomorrow. She said, "Sure!" He then explained that he had left a camera and several rolls of exposed films in a taxi in Hong Kong two days earlier. They were vital to the job he was on. He couldn't have them mailed because of the risk of delays in customs and damage to the camera and film. He could, however, send someone to get them. He was working with the rest of his photos and needed these within a week. Twenty-four hours later she landed in Hong Kong, the guest of the photographer's client, and of an airline and a hotel featured in the upcoming photo-essay. She enjoyed the sights for five days, flew home, to give him his film, his camera and her thanks.

The second story is about a woman who needed ten thousand dollars. She had incurred a once-in-a-lifetime expense, and her current job could not cover it. Around this time, she was asked to consult on a book in a specialized area for a modest fee. She did what was asked, sent it off, and forgot about it. Two weeks later, she went to New York on business. She decided to call the friend who had asked her to work on the book since he lived nearby. After tracking him by phone from his home to an office to a third location, she finally reached him in the apartment of the publisher of the proposed book. As they talked, the woman realized that she really could have done a better job had she known more about the book. She was willing to work with them that night, but she had no transportation; it was winter and it was late. She asked where they were and found that it was nearby. In fact it was the same building that she was calling from. It turned out to the one apartment in New York City that backed into a common back stairwell with the one she was in. Intrigued she crossed through the kitchen of one, through the hall, to the kitchen of the other. She met the publisher and suggested they review the structure of the proposed book. Before dawn they had completely reworked the book. The woman also secured a share of the royalties instead of a fee. When the book was published, it sold over 150,000 copies. Her share came to slightly over ten thousand dollars!

A DIRECT METHOD

Here is a simple, yet effective procedure to solve problems using your higher mind. Each step may produce a solution. If it does not, then proceed to the next step.

I. Define the problem as fully and correctly as possible.

This actually solves a number of problems which are obscure, vague or distorted. Writing down the problem tends to force you to clarify that part of the total situation which is the problem. If you say, "My daughter is a problem to me," that's vague and unspecific. If you reflect a moment then restate the problem as follows, "My daughter has begun to stay out so late on the weekends that she starts school worn out. Then her work slips. When that occurs she is prone to stay up late trying to catch up, and she consequently is sick a lot." Defining a problem as clearly as possible moves you that much closer to a solution or, at least,gives you an idea what direction to go toward finding a solution.

II. Get additional information.

Many problems need only a bit of new data, or an additional resource or a different expert before they can be solved. I tried for years to get one room of my home to be cooler in the summer. Finally I asked someone in the construction business. He suggested a very simple way to revent my attic which solved the problem. Don't be unwilling to ask for help; the world is full of solutions.

III. Redefine the problem to yourself, mentally.

With the new information and another try at definition, many more problems become obvious. Sometimes a problem will resolve itself by our understanding it more clearly. For example, all new parents know the relief of finding out that what they considered a major problem with their baby is only a stage in development. A problem redefined is easy to live with.

IV. Ask yourself, your whole self, to consider the problem and to offer you a solution.

This triggers the higher self and begins a process which, although too complex to discuss here, allows your own inner voice to speak to you. People who work this way get their answers from dreams or occasionally from a literal voice. This is a phenomenon that we observed in our review of composers, writers and inventors.

V. Turn your conscious awareness to other activities.

Why this is necessary is not at all clear. It is as if the higher mind does not function if the usual conscious mind is working on the problem. It is like a parent who will not help a child while the child is struggling with a problem. Only after the problem has clearly overwhelmed the child does the parent step in and present another way.

Some people speak of this as turning their problem over to a higher power. What happens is clear; how it occurs is still a mystery. The ancient Greeks depicted the various creative arts as Goddesses who looked with favor on individuals who would then have the ability to create works of great beauty. Our contemporary psychological suggestions are no more illuminating and not at all as attractive as the earlier Greek speculations.

* * * *

We have briefly examined a few ways to develop and enrich our own capabilities. We know that we can improve our possibilities. We also know that if we wish to improve, and we have the knowledge, we can improve. We enjoy expanding our skills. Problem solvers are among the happiest people I know. They delight in stretching their minds past their prior limits; they delight in creating their own future. As we considered the basic goals of western civilization, we saw that health, and family were as important as career and income, perhaps more so. Now that we have discussed the fully functioning mind, and more than a few ways to solve problems, let us turn to an examination of basic issues that relate to improved health and a loving family environment.

VII

HEALTH

Our most fundamental need is good health. As infants our first desires are to be fed, warm, comfortable, and free from pain. While we are young, we expect good health. As we grow older, have accidents, contract diseases, and stress ourselves, we realize that our health is our responsibility and under our control. We can improve our health.

The research findings are clear:

Hard-driving, active executives die young.

He who sleeps little doesn't last long.

Those who ignore the body may not live to regret it.

Relaxation prolongs your life.

We need to acknowledge the basic facts; most of us allow too many pressures into our lives. We justify the discomfort we feel because we believe we have no alternative. It is true that we need a certain amount of challenge and surprise; we also need to push our limits to be fully human. Too much hurts us, too little weakens us. Like athletes who alternate between hard training, easy training and rests, we need to be able to shift our own patterns so that we can take on more, become healthier, rest more fully, and recover more swiftly.

Look at your life carefully. Can you identify situations where tensions accumulate? Can you do something to change these situations? Reducing tensions is a housekeeping job. It is like trimming ivy off the paths in a garden. You trim so that you can enjoy the pleasure of clear walks. The ivy, however, continues to grow so that new leaves soon crowd the same path. Effective pruning is done on a regular basis. Good health is a set of habits, not a series of events. If you treat your body as a friend and cater to its needs, it will reward you with long life. Treat it like a pack horse; overload it with the bulky gear of your career, and it may collapse under you.

THE MIND-BODY CONNECTION

The mind directly influences the body. When we watch a frightening film, the body reacts with fear. When we see an erotic photograph, the body reacts sexually. The body also directly influences the mind. You can be having a wonderful conversation, but should your head throb or your stomach cramp, the conversation will lose its luster. If you become preoccupied with physical pain, your mental health suffers.

Mental imagery creates a curious interaction between body and mind. You not only have a physical body but you also have, in your mind, a mental image of your body. Usually the two overlap tightly, but you can separate the image from the physical at will with training and to your advantage.

Carl Simonton's initial work, which was described earlier in these pages, determined that when patients consciously create an image body that was healthier than their physical body, their health improved. If your body image is less healthy than your body, your health will decline. Startling evidence includes

112

alleged "talking deaths." In these cases a powerful figure, usually a medicine man or shaman, publicly tells a person that he or she will become ill and die. The person begins to sicken, and within a short time actually dies. This can occur when a Western doctor looks up from your medical tests and charts and tells you that you will not get better, and that you have only so many months left to live. A strong enough belief in the doctor's wisdom lowers the "will to live." Also, in a striking study of the placebo effect, a group of patients was told that the drug they were given was a new form of chemotherapy. Forty percent of the group suffered hair loss. The drug was, in fact, milk sugar. The medicine man is a powerful authority figure in hospitals or in tribal gatherings.

We can learn to work with images of ourselves to maintain a high-level of health. Using positive imaging to improve performance has been part of my training since the early sixties. A few sports professionals started to work with it in the seventies and the ideas became widely accepted at the Los Angeles Olympic Games of 1984. A number of athletes who were recovering from operations or injuries which by conventional medical standards should have sidelined them completely, won medals in those games. Mental imaging helped them control their bodies in spite of their physical "limitations."

Sports medicine and sports psychology are studying not only the prevention of disease and the elimination of symptoms, but also ways in which already successful, healthy, aware, and motivated individuals can continue to improve. Time spent learning imaging techniques can benefit anyone's long-term health. It is not limited to athletes or to athletic performance. Which techniques you choose to learn will depend on your goals. The methods are only now beginning to get the wide-spread attention they deserve. From arthritis to diabetes, from cancer to the common cold, from walking to sky-diving, from weight lifting to fly-casting, imaging helps overcome limitations and improve your vitality.

STRESS AND CHANGE

To promote the intertwining of success, improved health and increased leisure, we need to understand the relationships between change, stress, and illness.

The research of Thomas Holmes has been invaluable for understanding the critical effects of stress. Holmes made two connected discoveries. First, the more changes there are in your life, the greater the likelihood of serious physical illness. Holmes computed the relative magnitude or seriousness of various life changes, giving a number of points to each (see table). As the total number of points increased, **irrespective of the kind of change**, the probability of serious illness also increased. What is striking is that negative events and positive ones **both** add to total stress. For example, divorce is a high stress event (63 points), as is being fired from work (47 points). However, marriage is also a stressful event (50 points), as is retirement (45 points).

From the body's point of view, a change is a change is a change. Too many changes exceed the body's capacity to adapt to new demands. A similar finding links major life events to weight gains. In overweight people, during stressful periods, weight goes up, and after the stress is over, the weight remains.

These findings caused me to reflect about the impact of the Omega seminar as well as other work in which I was involved. The research on Omega graduates shows that over half undergo major changes in their lives in the first few years following the seminar. Income goes up (38 points on the Holmes scale), couples buy a larger home (20 points) with a larger mortgage (31 points). People take more vacations (13 points), sometimes change jobs (36 points), become pregnant (40 points), and achieve outstanding personal success (28 points). Was this work not only aiding people in garnering successes but also setting them up for major illnesses?

Table 23.2
The Social Readjustment Rating Scale

Life Event	Mean Value
1. Death of spouse	100
2. Divorce	73
3. Marital separation from mate	65
4. Detention in jail or other institution	63
5. Death of a close family member	63
6. Major personal injury or illness	53
7. Marriage	50
8. Being fired at work	47
9. Marital reconciliation with mate	45
10. Retirement from work	45
11. Major change in the health or behavior of a family member	44
12. Pregnancy	40
13. Sexual difficulties	39
14. Gaining a new family member (e.g., through birth, adoption, oldster moving in, etc.)	39
15. Major business readjustment (e.g., merger, reorganization, bankruptcy, etc.)	39
16. Major change in financial state (e.g., a lot worse off or a a lot better off than usual)	38
17. Death of a close friend	37
18. Changing to a different line of work	36
19. Major change in the number of arguments with spouse (e.g., either a lot more or a lot less than usual regarding childrearing, personal habits, etc.)	35
20. Taking on a mortgage greater than $10,000 (e.g., purchasing a home, business, etc.)	31
21. Foreclosure on a mortgage or loan	30
22. Major change in responsibilities at work (e.g., promotion, demotion, lateral transfer)	29
23. Son or daughter leaving home (e.g., marriage, attending college, etc.)	29
24. In-law troubles	29
25. Outstanding personal achievement	28
26. Wife beginning or ceasing work outside the home	26
27. Beginning or ceasing formal schooling	26

Table 23.2
The Social Readjustment Rating Scale (Cont.)

Life Event	Mean Value
28. Major change in living conditions (e.g., building a new home, remodeling, deterioration of home or neighborhood)	25
29. Revision of personal habits (dress, manners, associations, etc.)	24
30. Troubles with the boss	23
31. Major change in working hours or conditions	20
32. Change in residence	20
33. Changing to a new school	20
34. Major change in usual type and/or amount of recreation	19
35. Major change in church activities (e.g., a lot more or a lot less than usual)	19
36. Major change in social activities (e.g., clubs, dancing, movies, visiting, etc.)	18
37. Taking on a mortgage or loan less than $10,000 (e.g., purchasing a car, TV, freezer, etc.)	17
38. Major change in sleeping habits (a lot more or a lot less sleep, or change in part of day when asleep)	16
39. Major change in number of family get-togethers (e.g., a lot more or a lot less than usual)	15
40. Major change in eating habits (a lot more or a lot less food intake, or very different meal hours or surroundings)	15
41. Vacation	13
42. Christmas	12
43. Minor violations of the law (e.g., traffic tickets, jaywalking, disturbing the peace, etc.)	11

Source: Holmes, T. H., and Rahe, R. H. The Social Readjustment Rating Scale. Journal of Psychosomatic Research, 1967. 11 213-218.

What we found matched Holmes' second finding. He observed that the grim correlations between stress and illness were true **only if people were unaware of the relationship between**

change-events and their own health. Awareness of the links between change, stress, and illness could turn the correlations around. Holmes published a list of preventive measures to counterbalance stressful changes and for the "maintenance of your health and the prevention of illness." He suggested that we become familiar with what change-events are and the amount of impact they can have, then to "think about different ways you might best adjust to the event." In my work, I concluded that one of the necessary basic changes to encourage is **improving overall health** by balancing each additional life change with appropriate physical improvements. Techniques, now offered during the seminar and available in other forms, become basic habits necessary for health enhancement as well as specific ways to reduce tension.

As we have learned, much of our early childhood is spent responding to the suggestions of our parents. Many of those suggestions, direct and indirect, are instrumental in the development of our personality. By working directly with the words and images that have the most profound effects on children I found that adults can consciously reorient their systems so that long-term chronic disabilities begin to heal. For example, a Catholic nun had suffered for years from allergies and carried with her a pouch of antihistamines, Kleenex, and nasal sprays. During a seminar she learned a technique that brought her almost instant relief. She continued to refine that technique and, for the past fifteen years, has been symptom free.

We no longer divide illness into "physical" or "mental". Every illness is part of a larger syndrome which includes the physical, social, environmental, psychological and spiritual dimensions of the individual. When we are in pain it is unimportant to us whether the primary cause is physical, mental, emotional, or environmental. The pain is a reality.

Some people use techniques to obtain immediate symptomatic relief. Others discover new ways to work on their physical conditions. One graduate, for example, became a serious long-distance runner. Unfortunately, he became aware of irregularities in his heart beat as he pushed himself to new personal records. A cardiologist checked him and while he found no physical damage, he advised him to give up his running. This person didn't wish to accept the advice. He decided to look more closely at what caused his heart to misfire since not every workout seemed to disturb it. He ran a number of different ways and found that one running pattern caused the heart irregularities every time. Satisfied with the solution he resumed his running and later sought out coaching from a professional who gave him alternative ways to do his workouts. The irregularities ceased and he continued to progress in both running and general health.

THE POWER OF WORDS

What is it about words that gives them such power? The Christian story of creation begins, "In the beginning was the Word, and the Word was with God and the Word was God." Some Christian traditions relate that Jesus knew the "words of power" that could heal the sick and even raise the dead. A provocative viewpoint is found in the cosmology of some African tribes who believe that the entire universe is a living being. Everything has a living, active core. Thus people, animals, plants, thunderstorms, mountains, and rivers are all alive, each in its way. Words too are alive, being part of the creation. Since words are alive they can have power. Since we know that words do have power, we can see how these tribes concluded that they are alive. We should all use words carefully. We know, for example, that some words are not to be spoken aloud within some groups. "Don't say that" is a common request. We also have traditions of protecting ourselves after we say certain words. We cross ourselves, knock on wood, spit, or say a prayer. All these old forms acknowledge the vital power of words.

According to some African beliefs, one power evoked by words is that of making a wish. There is an inherent power in the words to bring the wish into reality. Affirmations are a Western version of this idea. Research into childhood shows that the power of words is stronger in childhood than at any other time. However, words continue to affect us throughout our lives. Studies have shown that patients undergoing surgery with full anesthesia not only can hear what is being said, but react to it directly and physically following the operation. Research also confirms that patients who were told during surgery that they would recover easily, with few complications, spent less time in intensive care and in the hospital overall than people who heard only music during a similar operation. The words we speak to ourselves are incorporated into our bodies as well as our minds. Therefore, it behooves us to notice and be careful what we say about our health. Prophecies can be curses or blessings, evoking the power of words to create personal health for better or worse. In the African world, curses are used consciously and directly to harm others. In the Christian world we bless buildings, boats, meals, and one another.

Look at the following sentences. Notice the different potential effects on your health if you tell yourself the following:

"As I get older, my eyesight is going to get worse and worse."

"Like my Dad always said, 'When you turn 40, your belt needs to get bigger to hold your belly.' "

"After childbirth, you can never lose all the weight you've gained."

Now consider these sentences:

"As I understand myself better, it gets easier and easier to

119

control my weight."

"My eyesight is improving."

"People my age get extra pleasure out of being in shape."

"I don't eat desserts very often any more, but when I do I really enjoy the treat."

We can use words to help ourselves or to harm ourselves. There is no more powerful tool so readily available to each of us as the words we speak on a daily basis.

THE PROBLEM OF PAIN

No one benefits from unnecessary pain. There are two general types of pain, immediate and chronic. Immediate pain is the body's early warning system. Touch your finger to a hot stove and before you know it is burning you your hand jerks itself away. Immediate pain protects the body. Chronic pain can result from injury or illness. When you sprain an ankle, it aches to remind you to put less weight on it until it heals.

Solely physical methods of treatment, primarily drugs and surgery, often are not effective. The pain signals seem to go around the physical gaps made by the surgery and overstep the dampening effects of pain killers. These methods may be temporary and even debilitating.

Pain clinics have been established that teach mental imaging, relaxation, and other alternative methods of pain control. Patients are taught to expand their physical self-control. They observe themselves closely, learning how many internal sensations can be controlled by training. They were taught to image their own bodies free of pain. In many cases the results were striking. One clinic reported on patients who, before coming to the clinic, had had an **average** of three or more operations for pain alone. After three weeks of intensive training, more than 60% of these patients were able to resume a full work, social, and

120

family life. These successes were characterized by the same qualities we saw in fine athletes or in groups of peak performers. Specifically, high self-concept, a strong belief in their own capacities, with a willingness, even a joy, in learning coupled with skill in imaging.

It is your body's goal to stay well. You can do a great deal to improve your health. Your mind may be excited when drunk, your ambition may feed on too much coffee, your social needs may keep you up to all hours, but your body, the beautiful package that your mind rides in, wishes only health. By aligning the goals of your mind with those of your body you can decrease tensions, minimize unnecessary pain and alleviate longstanding health conditions. Believing that a health problem can be solved is necessary before you can explore solutions. As your self-concept improves, so must your health.

A middle-aged carpenter was injured in a car accident. He listened when his physician told him that he could not expect a full recovery. He did not accept the diagnosis, and began to explore areas of physical training unknown to his physician. He found that he could get help, but that he had to learn to take more control of his own healing for it to be effective. After several years, he has full use of all his limbs and, "feels better than before the accident." Solutions to health problems arise from the same forces necessary to achieve other goals:

> Intention
> Information
> Practice
> Plan to be in good health
> Find out how
> Do it

Find ways you enjoy. The body is marvelously elastic. It can respond positively to rest, to effort, to passive work, to active work, to mental work, to food, and to environmental changes.

There is no one right way. Conventional medicine can often be exactly what you need. Conventional nutrition can also be exactly what you need. So may the wide, wonderful worlds of sports medicine, holistic health, and health psychology. You will find the way that is right for you. The body and the mind both love and support health.

A final story

I received a letter from a college woman who had heard a talk I gave about overcoming limitations. She wrote:

"I was really moved by your lecture ... the analogy to running had personal meaning to me because I've experienced success in running by shedding mental barriers. I'd never run more than three miles at a time and one day I entered a road race of four miles, primarily to get a free T-shirt. To my surprise I came in second and impressed a university cross county coach enough so he offered to coach me through the summer. He encouraged me to run farther than I'd ever imagined possible. In the winter I began to train for a marathon with some other people on the track team ... when I ran with them it was easy to say, 'if they can do it, so can I'. In the spring I ran the 26 mile race without stopping, and even though my time was slow, I was thrilled and ready to try another. (Marathons are great because they're not really races if you're not in the top ten. Everyone roots for everyone else and offers encouragement). I trained seriously in the summer for another marathon and got second place, demolishing my old time by a half-hour to run a 3:16. Elated by my marathon victory, I started cross country again. I knocked minutes off my 5000 meters time and was one of the fifteen runners in the Western Athletic Conference to qualify for the nationals in Florida ..."

"Anyway, in a little more than a year I went from running my first four mile race to two marathons to the cross country

122

nationals. I don't think I possess any great physical talents. I think I just got caught up in a catalytic group of runners. We pushed away one anothers' mental barriers of distance and time — a kind of positive peer pressure. I think anyone can finish a marathon. It's just a matter of convincing oneself that 5 miles, 10 miles, 20 miles are not impossible distances."

"No great physical talents." Perhaps that is so. What this young woman did have was motivation, acquired knowledge, practices, and the knowledge of how to set goals. She was in an environment which encouraged her to keep developing herself in the way she wished. Her story is a typical one of someone who allowed herself to get what she wanted. Her mind and body worked smoothly together to support her intentions.

VIII

MARRIAGE
AND
CHILDREN

A GOOD MARRIAGE IS THE HIGHEST ART

There is no reason why marriages should not be superb. My files are filled with letters that begin, "Our marriage was excellent before, but it is even more wonderful now."

Being productive, creative, and successful is of great value, yet other goals are equally compelling if not more important. Economic ease is not an end in itself; it is a foundation for a fuller life. Success that is limited to income, productivity, assets, and property is half-success. Full success includes the joys of good relationships with close friends and with parents, your spouse, and children. Without someone to share with and to give to, material goals lose their savor. There is no reason why our emotional partnerships should not be comforting and rewarding. There is no reason why such relationships should interfere with or restrict your other successes.

Once, while consulting with a company president, I laid out a proposal which allowed people a shorter work week. He looked at me and said, "I think you just want people to be happy. You don't give a damn about the bottom line." I replied, "If you don't think that happier, more comfortable people improve your bottom line, you don't know a thing about your bottom line." Together we created a shorter work week and a better bottom line.

It is valuable to review the state of our relationships when we establish new goals. Whenever any family member raises his or her self-concept, the emotional fabric of the family undergoes an expansion and a relaxation. When we create change in our lives, the dynamics of our marriage change. Understanding those dynamics can make that change a joy.

Marriage is your responsibility

Having spoken to hundreds of couples, I can safely say that most of them consciously know of a number of ways which could improve their marriage. In most cases each can see how the other could change and how that would make things better for both of them.

There is usually real caring, clear perception, and genuine compassion in those realizations.

"If she would only ..."

"If he could, just once ..."

Absolutely true, valid, and stabbingly accurate. Their suggestions are the right answers, but to the wrong question. It is not, "What can my spouse do to make our marriage better" but

"What can I do to improve our marriage?" The answers to that question come more slowly and with hesitation, as if by speaking out you compromise yourself. If you know what you might do to make it even better, your rational mind says, "Well then, why aren't you doing it?"

The answer is that we all could be doing better if there were not so many negative habits or fears inhibiting our willingness and capacity. It is our awareness of our own limits that makes us turn first to our spouse with a request that they change. We do not see their hidden limits as clearly as our own. We are not sure why they can't do what we would have them do. We know fully well why we can't do what they ask us to do. A lesson from the book **A Course in Miracles** says it well. "I am tempted to believe that I am upset because of what other people do, or because of circumstances and events which seem to be beyond my control. I may experience being upset as some form of anger, jealousy, resentment, depression. Actually all of these feelings represent some form of fear, and I have a choice ..."

As self-concept strengthens, we may confront problems that had previously gone unsolved. We have additional resources to bring about the desired resolution. We can correct the imbalances within ourselves, complete our childhood, and improve our marriage.

TOWARD A BETTER MARRIAGE

In buying real estate, they say there are three important considerations: location, location, and location. In marriage, there are also three considerations: communication, communication, and communication. Recent research done on thousands of marriages shows that a marriage was most likely to be seen as satisfying (to both partners) when communication was rated excellent. Communication was more important than financial, social, or even sexual compatability. Marriage, if not all relationships, follows the same general rules when it moves from constriction to freedom. What works includes the following:

Intention

When we make improving a relationship a goal, we put new energy into it. Most couples do not understand that maintaining a relationship is a continual, ongoing job of renewal. It is not a safe harbor, but an active voyage. Intention keeps our hands on the wheel so that as the winds change, we correct and improve on how we treat each other.

Believable hope

Observe those couples whose marriages are as happy as you intend yours to be. You can learn by observing successful, thriving, vibrant marriages. Marriage is an art which can be studied, practiced, refined, and studied some more. Each stage of life is different in a marriage. Become aware of what makes a marriage wonderful in the first flush of love, when children arrive, during the middle years of career change, as well as in the later years of children leaving, careers slowing, and in the final years of greatest quiet. Each period demands new skills, and evokes new levels of understanding concerning yourself and your spouse. Although marriage is not taught, it may still be learned.

Self-concept

How much happiness do you deserve? The more you are willing to have, the more you are likely to get. What are your own anticipations about your marriage? Do you envision it improving, staying the same, or even declining as the years go on? As in

128

other areas of our lives, we have a stock of beliefs about our relationships which affect us deeply. Here perhaps more than in any other part of our lives we need to sift our childhood observations and decisions from our adult desires and goals. As our self-concept matures, so will our relationships.

Using what you already know

Just as we know many ways in which we can improve our marriage and our other relationships, we need to be able to utilize what we know. If you feel blocked or unable to do what you know would help, then you can ask what else you need to learn. Your higher self is there to draw upon, as are all the other tools, guides, and information you need. If you have learned to ask for support, guidance and direction, then it will be given to you. If you have not learned it is still another goal to achieve. You can learn what you need to know.

Just as there are classes in childcare for prospective parents, there are learnable skills which help marriages work. What is wonderful about marriage is that there are ample opportunities to practice ways of relating that serve the marriage, as well as endless chances to stop habits which limit loving and cherishing one another.

Carl Rogers, in a book exploring marriage, concludes that the core of any long-term intimate relationship rests on a pledge, a commitment that certain elements will be true as often and as much as possible. He summarizes each element as an agreed-upon ideal for a continuing, beneficial, and meaningful relationship.

Rogers' pledges include:

Dedication of Commitment

"We each commit ourselves to working together on the changing process of our relationship, because that relationship is currently enriching our love and our life, and we wish it to grow."

Communication:
The expression and acceptance of feelings

"I will risk myself by endeavoring to communicate any persistent feeling, positive or negative, to my partner — to the full depth that I understand it in myself — as a living part of me. Then I will risk further by trying to understand, with all the empathy I can bring to bear, his or her response, whether it is accusatory and critical or sharing or self-revealing."

Nonacceptance of roles

"We will live by our own choices, the deepest organismic sensings of which we are capable, but we will not be shaped by the wishes, the rules, the roles which others are all too eager to thrust upon us."

Becoming a separate self

"... I can be a real member of a partnership, because I am on the road to being a real person. And I am hopeful that I can encourage my partner to follow his or her own road to a unique personhood, which I would love to share."

Rogers' understanding, gained from a lifetime of counseling, is that marriage is a living, active, daily activity. It works as well as we are willing to have it work. It flourishes under the watchful care of two people who have learned that the pleasure that comes from watching your partner grow is equal to or greater than your own pleasure. Like a team of matched horses, a good couple pulls their marriage smoothly and easily. Sensitive to each other's needs, they enjoy moving ahead together.

CHILDREN

Parents do the best job they possibly can to raise their children. Every parent gives all the love, all the support, all the teaching, and all the encouragement available to each child. Yet, most parents, in spite of these best efforts, have minor or major concerns about their children.

Although parents do the best job they can, they must acknowledge their limitations. **A child cannot receive more love than parents have to give. Parents cannot give more love to their children then they have for themselves. We cannot love others more than we love ourselves.** Any limitations or restrictions we have, from our own childhood or any other source, is replayed in our parenting and reemerges in our children. Similarly, any change in our level of self-acceptance will manifest itself in our children. Our children absorb our limits, our confusions, and our concerns. They also absorb our intentions, our capacities, and our strengths.

Children may be undernourished, not for food but for acceptance. Symptoms of "affection malnutrition" may be caused by social or family difficulties, problems in school, even ill health. However, it is important to note that rebellion, at home or at school, is not necessarily a symptom of a problem. If children rebel against stupidity, cruelty, rigidity, or unkindness at home or at school, such children are sound, self-reliant and determined to make their world a healthier one. If, however, children rebel against useful rules, genuine affection, and helpful support, then parents should rightfully be concerned.

What do children need?

love
attention
support
freedom

Love

Children's need for love is paramount. Studies done during World War II found that orphans given adequate food, shelter, warmth, and living facilities sickened, became crippled, suffered mental problems and died far more often than other orphans given similar material support but who were also given affection, cuddling, and time with loving adults. Children thrive given enough of that invisible, pervasive vitamin we call love.

It is critical to recognize that love is fundamental and that from the source of love flows the rest of child rearing. Moreover, it is not the amount, but the quality of love that nourishes. Love is not measured with a stopwatch or a soup spoon, but by the way a child feels with or without it. Children have a vast capacity to absorb and accept love.

Love is neither discipline nor permissiveness; it is neither an act nor an activity; it is accepting another absolutely, without reservation, without demanding anything in return. As a recent mother said to me, "Some afternoons I get to love my baby daughter for hours at a time. She takes long naps so that nothing comes between me and loving her."

Attention

Attention is the second basic need in children. Adults demand attention just as much as children, but they are able to seek it for themselves. Children are small and unable to come and go when or where they choose. Adult attention is important so that children know that they exist as their own person. What they say, think, or do is real to them and needs a response. "Children should be seen but not heard" is bad advice. Children should be seen, heard, and attended to.

Giving attention to a child does not mean giving agreement. It is not necessarily doing what the child wishes; it is not equated with playing, reading, or any other particular activity. It is rather, clearly noticing and reacting to what a child is doing, planning, thinking, and saying.

If you have ever watched a child talking to a parent while

132

the parent reads the paper, you have seen an example of lack of attention. Contrast that with a child on a swing, swinging as high as they dare, joyfully crying out "look-a-me, look-a-me" to a parent who follows every swing. Attention lets your children know that you are in contact, that you care and that they matter.

We all prefer positive attention, but we still do well even when some attention is negative. If children do not get enough attention by being well-behaved, polite, and good in school, they may try to gain the necessary attention by being rude and rowdy, by being troublesome, by performing poorly in school, or by acting out at home. Their goal is to get more attention, even if it involves being punished. What is often labeled "bad behavior" is often simply a plea for more attention.

Support

Support, the third need, is part love and part attention yet it is a different quality than either. To support children it is necessary to assure them and encourage them to be in touch with their own special qualities so they may learn, stumble, experiment — without fearing the withdrawal of love or the loss of attention. The most substantial families have children who were encouraged to explore their worlds as widely as possible, and to have as rich and complex a childhood as safety and health allows. For this children need to consciously experience parental support.

If you observe families with children who are doing remarkable things for their age in almost every case you will find parents who support the activity with time, energy, and if necessary, economic sacrifices. More often than not the activity is one that the parents are interested in as well. Thus the child is not only supported but tutored as well. Childhood musicians often come from families who play and practice together. Fine athletes often have athletic parents. Children who are excellent with animals usually come from farm families or families with many pets.

133

Writers produce writers; chefs grow up with chefs; daredevils have parents as bold as they are. Parents who give their children adequate support produce children willing to excel. The kind and amount of support we can offer our children as they learn determines the quality of their eventual performance.

With sufficient support children discover that any developed skill boosts their overall competence, raises their self-concept and fosters their interest in other areas. Studies following gifted children over forty years have found that good qualities cluster together. For example, children who are bright academically are also likely to be excellent athletically, attractive socially, and good musically. The stereotypes of the rigid engineer, the empty-headed beauty, or the socially inept class brain are exceptions. Given enough support children become generally proficient. Much of the joy of parenting comes from relishing the continuing effects of early support.

Freedom

Freedom is the fourth basic childhood need and in many ways the most difficult to foster. Children are not free. They are not little angels come to earth. They are small, physically slight, powerless beings living in the homes of large, powerful parents who can control and influence their every activity. From waking to eating to dressing to learning to sleeping, children have little personal freedom.

As parents, we walk a tightrope between excessive control and excessive freedom. On one side, we teach, demand, make rules, and reward specific behavior. At the same time we allow and encourage freedom, permitting children to make their own choices and decisions, and to chart their own pathways. If we can keep in mind that our goal is **not** to produce obedient, placid, well-mannered adults, but to encourage powerful, effective, independent, sensitive, sensible, and creative adults, then we shall remain sensitive to the tightrope.

I recall a time when my two daughters first visited my parents in Los Angeles on their own. They were young and often unruly. After the trip my father spoke to me about their table manners. He was impressed at how polite, how delicate, and how proper they were at every meal. Not having seen too much of that behavior at home, I asked them how they came to be such models when they were with their grandparents. They both giggled and poked each other. "We made a game out of it," said the younger. "And we knew it mattered to them," added the elder. They had enough skill to be mannered when a situation called for it. They were using their freedom. Good behavior was one but certainly not their only choice.

Freedom is the ability to choose in the moment what is best for us to do. Capacity is the ability to do what we choose. Therefore it is as important for children to have a wide range of choices as it is for them to behave themselves. My teenage daughter was standing in a subway train and felt a boy about her own age press against her. As she moved away from him she saw his hand was in her purse. She turned and punched him — hard, in the chest. Her friends were aghast since all they saw was their usually well-mannered friend turn and hit a stranger. The pickpocket turned and fled. That was not polite behavior, but it was the right behavior at the time. Freedom for our children is the capacity and flexibility to respond fully to opportunities, difficulties, and pleasures.

Well-meaning parents often cut subtle yet deep inroads into their children's self-concept. For example, a woman in her early sixties worked with me to discover what lay behind her excessive fear of falling down either physically, mentally, or emotionally. All her adult life she had worried whether she was doing a good enough job or whether she was "falling down on the job." She had even avoided sports with her children because she might fall while playing. Finally, she dredged up memories of learning to walk. She had been born prematurely. Her parents were extremely careful with her as a result. Thus when she began to walk her mother was always there supporting her, even putting pillows beside her to cushion her falls. What she learned (while learning to walk) was that when she fell she frightened mother. Therefore, "to fall" was dangerous. As a child and as an adult, she was careful about any form of falling; falling behind in class, falling from grace, falling in play, and falling in love. Once she understood that her fear of falling and her negative habit patterns around falling arose from her early childhood experiences and from the good will of her parents, she began to release those nagging concerns that had troubled her all her life.

Another women was working on a carpentry project with me. She became frustrated when she was unable to nail a board into a corner. The nails kept bending and she started to cry from exasperation. Then she became hysterical, fearful, and began to choke. I took her to a quiet spot where I helped her follow her fear and choking into early memories. She recalled that her father became very upset when she cried. Sometimes, when she could not stop crying he would grab her throat to stifle her tears. She learned that crying led to being choked, to not being able to breathe. Therefore to cry felt terribly dangerous. Her father didn't understand what he was doing and neither did she. The results restricted her emotional life and affected her job, her marriage, and to a lesser extent, her own children.

It is said, with irony, that childhood is too dangerous for children. It is a time of wonder, of love, of discovery, but it is also a time of doubts, fears and dangers. Children need protection.

Once, I was up on a roof with a friend and his four year old son. As we climbed down a ladder to the ground, the boy did it with some help and with great care. When he made it to the ground, he was pleased with himself. His father was proud of him and said, "That was good. You are a big boy now." The child turned and looked up, way up, at his father who towered over him. "No I'm not," he said, "I'm very little."

Children are little and do get afraid. They are afraid they may not get food, or sleep, or relief from pain. They are most afraid that their parents might not love them enough. Common signs of childhood anxieties include fingernail biting, thumb-sucking, the need for a blanket, or a stuffed toy. All these are normal responses to a world filled with unknowns. Before you consider separating a child from a favorite blanket, remember that it may be his/her very real defense against anxiety, just as a lucky piece or a religious medal may be an adult's. We all want to be secure and protected from the unknown. As we release some of their own childhood-generated fears, our children's anxieties will diminish.

A basic shift occurs when parents enjoy themselves and their children more. The best possible help you can give to your young children is to become a happier, freer, healthier person yourself. You serve your child first as a parent and second as a model. An Omega graduate started to show her new attitude and used some new ways with her children. Within a week, both of her children were feeling more relaxed and their relationship with each other had improved. One afternoon she overheard the youngest trying the new techniques on their family dog, attempting to correct his misbehavior as her own had been helped.

I once asked a high school girl why she was so intent on taking this seminar. She replied, "Anything that can make my Mom change so much and be a better Mom is powerful stuff. I want it for myself."

Children and School

Apart from parents, school is the most important influence in a child's life. From nursery school through graduate school, opportunities abound to develop or crush a child's full potential. What can parents do to improve the school experience? The answer, from school teachers, administrators and boards of education, is to support your children, the teachers, and the school.

Support your child

Most teachers are interested in doing the best job they can for your child. The more you support their efforts, the more they will support your child. **Visit your child's teachers.** Not with problems or concerns or requests; not even with ideas ... but to meet them and to introduce yourself as a parent who cares. Your visible interest in your children and your interest in their teachers will help. Teachers are no different from the rest of us in that they respond to attention and to appreciation. They intend to do well. Let them know you will help them if you can. Being a fine school teacher is not an easy job.

I asked a junior high school teacher how he felt about parents who called him or visited him. His answer was sobering. "I teach almost two hundred children a day. The school's crowded, and we're understaffed. Last year, two sets of parents spoke to me about their children. I still remember those two kids."

Letting a teacher know that you are actually interested in your children's development, not just their grades, gives a teacher unusual support. It is puzzling why so many parents rarely talk with the teachers directly. Your child may tell you that it is embarrassing and that no one else's parents do it. That may be true, and is all the more reason for you to reach out to your children's teachers.

Support the teacher

A single teacher can leaven an entire school. A nun who taught in a tough inner-city school learned Omega's ideas over her summer vacation. On her return, she was given a class of the most feared kids in the school. On the first day of class, almost every child carried a weapon but after four weeks the last weapon disappeared. By Christmas break the class was singing together. She sent me a tape of the class singing an original song of their own titled, "I Like Myself." I have heard better voices, but no sweeter music. Another high school teacher trained in self-concept work, asked for and was given the hard-core class; those students who were too disruptive for most classes. Needless to say their grades were among the worst in the school. After one year that class scored at the **top** of the school in their academic subjects.

Children whose self-concept is supported by teachers and parents improve in school. They direct their incredible store of energy towards substantial, life-affirming goals.

Support the school

It **is** possible to integrate the principles described in this book in schools and school districts.

How good can a school be? It can be a place much like one school near my home where there are excellent relations between teachers and students, high academic test results without expensive supplemental programs, and where the equipment and grounds are cared for by the students and staff. It can be a place where children weep before vacations, and cry again at the end of the school year. "School makes me feel good all over. I don't want a vacation," sobbed a fifth grader in one of these schools. Graduates of this school regularly become leaders in the local high schools that they scatter to. The core belief of this school is a high regard for the integrity and individuality of each student. The teachers have learned to structure the school for freedom and to give each child love, attention, support, and opportunities.

The lesson from this school is that the children will learn if we let them; that they have an innate drive to master their world and will do so in a school that respects and allows this drive to flourish.

In Fairmont, Minnesota, the superintendent wanted to impact the whole school system, city-wide, with the basic ideas taught in this book. A day was set aside by decree as "I LIKE MYSELF DAY." It was to be an in-service day for training. All the children in the city were released from school, and all the teachers and staffs convened at the one high school for a day of workshops that included grammar school teachers, junior high school teachers and the high school teachers. The Catholic and the Lutheran schools joined in as well. Not only were the teachers involved but there were workshops for the administration, library, cafeteria, and custodial staffs. The superintendent's intention was to have a school district where every member encouraged the development of every child and every other staff member.

The goals, as outlined in his memo to all school staff members, were as follows:

1. To help all staff members further identify with the district's goal of raising the self-concept of students.

2. To convince staff and parents that the process of raising self-concept is best implemented within a framework of good discipline and mutual respect for one another.

3. To learn specific ways for raising one's own self-concept and those around us.

The day did not revolutionize education in Fairmont. The system was already doing a good job. What was done was to introduce many of the ideas found within this book in such a way that the natural desire of teachers and staff to develop children was clarified and supported. The results included lower rates of vandalism, higher scores on state examinations, fewer absences for both teachers and students, and increased civic pride in the schools.

The self-concept of a child is far more flexible than in an adult. It is easier to raise a child's self-concept; there are fewer years of negative habit patterns which weigh it down. In our work I speak of "releasing a child's self-concept." Once parents and school allow the natural forces in their children free play, the rise in self-concept is swift and automatic.

Children are also easily wounded by the verbal assaults of adults. Untreated, these wounds lower self-concept in one area or another. If you ask a group of your friends to talk about some of the skills they never developed: art, music, dance, or writing, you will hear stories of a parent or teacher who said that their work was not any good — and that is why they had stopped producing it. I cringe when I hear of school teachers who have told small children that their pictures "don't look real," or "doesn't look like the one on the board" and as a result the children stop drawing. Yet, a stunted self-concept can be restored; creativity can be re-ignited.

One year on the first day of class and without any warning I asked my Stanford engineering students to compose a twelve line poem about love. From their upset reaction you might have thought I had asked them to tear their fingernails out. No one in that class had written a poem since grade school. Their poems were subsequently reviewed by a popular and charismatic member of the English faculty. She came to the class and read some of the best poems aloud, commenting on them and sharing her excitement about their work. By the end of the semester and without any further input, the students whose work had been singled out had written additional poems. Being encouraged allowed the students the freedom to explore parts of their own minds which had been closed off years earlier.

We are radiant beings! Look into any infant's eyes and you see pure potential. Our children do not lose their capacities, nor do we. That full potential can be re-established in families, in classrooms, and in whole school systems. It is a great pleasure not only to reach for the stars, but to encourage our children to reach with us. Their delight and yours is what this book is all about.

IX

AN END AND A BEGINNING

The primary purpose of this book had been to remind you of your potential and to augment your growth. While there has been advice in some areas, and specific recommendations in others, this is not a cookbook. This book gives only the first few crucial handholds for the climb to a better life. Each foot you rise reveals more sky, more trees, and more flowers. As you climb, you can hear more clearly the sounds of others ahead of you, wishing you their strength and their flexibility so that you may join them. This book is another step in your personal journey.

WHAT TO DO NOW

Now that you have read this book, what can you do? Here are several suggestions; evaluate them. Each is a different way to use what you may have gained. Each will augment and further

143

your personal power. They will help you get closer to what you are entitled.

Evaluate your home and your work

Look carefully at your own situation. Does it support the highest and best in you? Does your job encourage you to develop new skills? Does your work, your home, and your neighborhood make you comfortable? Does your spouse enjoy your good qualities and assist you to temper your faults? Is your environment physically healthy? Can you rely on your friends? Do your children have friends and a school that support the values you want them to develop?

If your answer to any of these questions is "no," then look at what is wrong for you. Once observed, you can take steps to improve it. There is no rule in this life that we must suffer. To the extent you control your days, they should reflect back a life of challenge and satisfaction. If it is not working, change it! You are the most powerful force in your life.

Make some changes

We thrive on a mixture of variety and stability. It is periodically valuable to take some area in your life and, by an act of will, change it. For example, the past decade has been one in which millions of us changed our leisure to include more active sports or more exercise. Those who made the change have enjoyed the benefits.

John Barth created a character in his book, **The End of the Opera**, who now and then would break one of his habits "just for the exercise of habit-breaking." It is a healthy exercise. It reminds us that we have a will, and that we have the capacity to overrule or restructure our habits should we choose to.

Get more information and life experience

There exist many opportunities to learn. With adult education, university extension courses, church-sponsored classes, retreats, growth centers, management courses, correspondence courses, travel and learning adventures, we float in a sea of potential learning. Be open to the courses taught near you and for you. It may be true that a little knowledge is a dangerous thing, but it is a higher truth that education makes your world richer and more extensive. It gives you more of life to work with in your pursuit of happiness.

This book grew out of one such course. In writing it I have been inspired by the diversity of ways to proceed from these ideas towards specific goals. Once attuned to their own goals people are amazed at the easy availability of opportunities

Observe those you respect

In American Indian lore there is a saying, "Do not judge another man until you have walked a mile in his moccasins." When you are with a person you respect or admire observe them closely. What is it that holds your attention? Is it their behavior, their mood, their bearing or the way they relate to others? What can you learn from others?

Individuals or couples can be models for your own goals. Once you observe something you like in another, see if you can uncover how he or she developed that capacity. When we see a friend with a new outfit, we ask where they found it. When we see a colleague with a new piece of equipment, we ask how well it works. We can ask friends about their cheerfulness, their easygoing children, their promotion, or their weight loss. They will be abundant and generous in their answers. There will always be those who know more than we do about those very things that we need to learn. Seek teachers or authors who will show you more truth. Remember that the test of a teacher or of a teaching is not what is promised or what is presented, but what is delivered. Test the results in yourself.

Look into your spiritual tradition

Most of us received the bulk of our religious training in Sunday School. Too many of us still think of our own spiritual background in childlike, over-simplified terms. Rarely have we fully explored the complexities, the depths, and the brilliance within our traditions.

What is clear from the opinions of the ordained ministers and theologians of many denominations with whom I've worked is that this book is aligned with the basic spiritual ideas which underlie most religious traditions. A young devout couple were sent to me by their company. They were a bit disturbed during the first two days of my teaching these ideas. They spoke to others, concerned that the teachings might be the work of the devil. As that seminar continued, they exchanged relieved looks and finally took me aside. They spoke of their fears and distrust of this material which initially seemed to oppose their own fundamental truths. Now they had a request. "Would you consider teaching a special seminar just for our church?" I answered that it was their task to understand the material well enough so that they could integrate it into their own religious framework and teach it if they wished. From that moment on, I never had more diligent or probing students.

It behooves us to glean spiritual understanding where we can. A good place to begin is with the spiritual tradition we know best. As the English mystic Evelyn Underhill said, "If God is infinite, then he can be apprehended in an infinite number of ways."

Enjoy yourself

This is the last and the most important suggestion. If you are not enjoying yourself, you are not doing a good job for

146

yourself, your company or your family.

A corporation, which was formed to deal with the flood of opportunities that followed a best selling book, adopted a set of corporate goals. These were formally decided, printed and distributed to each employee.

There were only three of these goals. The first two covered profitability and quality. The last one was "TO HAVE FUN." The president concluded when he established the company that if he and his employees were not having fun then something would have slipped away from the fundamental thrust of the company.

I have incorporated that goal into my working philosophy. It serves as an inner quality control for me and my clients with new programs, new staff, new facilities, and new levels of responsibility. It serves as a warning when things are beginning to freeze up at work or within any part of the organization. When someone comes to me and says, "You know my job isn't any fun any more," we sit down together and evaluate the job, the person, their career plans and the company's needs. We work on the problem until it is resolved in everyone's favor. High self-concept people support one another. It is a natural reaction when you have learned there is enough for everyone.

It is good business to have a good time.

LAST WORDS

This book, like you, is in the process of becoming. In a few years it will be rewritten, clarified, improved and issued afresh. Please help me with your comments, suggestions, criticisms and discoveries. You are the resource for every word.

147

SELECTED REFERENCES

Adams, James. **Conceptual Blockbusting**. Stanford Alumni
    Association, Stanford, California, 1974.

Assagioli, Roberto. **Psychosynthesis: A Manual of Principles
    and Techniques**. Penguin, New York, 1971.

Assagioli, Roberto. **The Act of Will**. Viking Press,
    New York, 1973.

A Course in Miracles, Foundation for Inner Peace,
    Tiburon, California, 1975.

Barth, John. **The Floating Opera**. Avon Books, New York, 1956.

Bandler, Richard & Grinder, John. **The Structure of Magic,
    Volume 1**. Science and Behavior,
    Palo Alto, California, 1976.

Brown, Molly Young. **The Unfolding Self**.
    Psychosynthesis Press. Los Angeles, 1983.

Cameron-Bandler, Leslie. **They Lived Happily Ever After**.
    Meta Publications, Cupertino, California, 1978.

Fadiman, James. "You and Your Attitudes" in **You Are
    Somebody Special**. Charlie Shedd, (Ed.), McGraw-Hill,
    New York, 1982, pp. 37-59.

Ferrucci, Piero. **What We May Be**. Tarcher, Los Angeles, 1982.

Frager, Robert & Fadiman, James. **Personality and Personal
    Growth**. (2nd Ed.) Harper and Row, New York, 1984.

Holmes, Thomas H. Stress: The New Etiology. in **Health for the
    Whole Person**. Hastings, A; Fadiman, J. & Gordon, J. (Eds)
    Westview Press, Boulder, Colorado, 1980. pp. 345-362.

Holmes, Thomas, H. & Rahe, R.H. The Social Readjustment
    Rating Scale. **Journal of Psychosomatic Research**,
    1967, 11, 213-218.

Horney, Karen. Finding the real self. **American Journal of
    Psychoanalysis**, 1949, 9:3.

Interaction Associates. **Strategy Notebook: Tools for Change**.
    Interaction, San Francisco, 1972.

James, William. **The Principles of Psychology**.
Holt, Reinehart, and Winston, New York, 1890.

James William, **Talks to Teachers**. Holt, Reinehart, and
Winston, New York, 1899.

James, William. **The Energies of Men**. Dodd, Mead and
Company, New York, 1926.

James, William. **Varieties of Religious Experience**.
Mentor, New York, 1958.

Lowry, R. (Ed.) **Dominance, Self-esteem, Self-actualization:
Germinal Papers of A.H. Maslow**. Brooks/Cole,
Monterey, California, 1973.

Maslow, A.H. **Toward a Psychology of Being**. Van Nostrand,
New York, 1968.

Maslow, A.H. **Motivation and Personality** (3rd Ed.).
Harper and Row, 1978.

Orage, A.R. **Psychological Exercises and Essays**.
Janus, London, 1965.

O'Regan, Brendan. **Personal Communication**. Institute of
Noetic Sciences, Sausalito, California, 1985.

Rogers, Carl. **On Becoming A Person**. Houghton Mifflin,
Boston, 1961.

Rogers, Carl. **Carl Rogers on Encounter Groups**.
Harper and Row, New York, 1970.

Rogers, Carl. **Becoming Partners: Marriage and Its Alternatives**.
Dell (Delacorte), New York, 1972.

Rosen, Sidney. **My Voice Will Go with You: The Teaching Tales
of Milton Erikson**. Norton, New York, 1982.

Simonton, Carl, Simonton, Stephanie, & Craig. **Getting Well
Again**. Tarcher, Los Angeles, 1981.

THE OMEGA SEMINAR

The ideas in this book are derived from the original work of John and Helen Boyle.

Their ideas are embodied in the teaching programs of Omega Seminars, Inc. Seminars are given in the United States and abroad for individuals, groups, and corporations. Special seminars can be given for any other interest group.

The seminars teach specific techniques to establish and to achieve definite and observable goals. Over the past 28 years, these seminars have been improved and developed to insure the subsequent success of the participants.

* * * *

If you wish information on the seminar itself, its results, or how you may attend, please send a postcard to:

OMEGA
2135 112th Ave. NE
Suite 102
Bellevue, Washington 98004

(206) 451-7477